To Darling Mark.
Dedicated to the Lord.
Sunday. 11TH September. 1994.

FROM. Great Granny Smith.
With lots of Love.

THE GOSPEL OF MARK ILLUMINATED

Published by
Lion Publishing plc
Sandy Lane West, Oxford, England
ISBN 0 7459 1440 3
Lion Publishing Corporation
1705 Hubbard Avenue, Batavia, Illinois 60510, USA
ISBN 0 7459 1440 3
Albatross Books Pty Ltd
PO Box 320, Sutherland, NSW 2232, Australia
ISBN 0 7324 0241 7

First edition 1990

British Library Cataloguing in Publication Data
[Bible. N.T. Mark. English. New International. 1990] The
Gospel of Mark illuminated.
 1. Bible. N.T. Mark. English. New International—Texts
 I. Nicholls, Rex   II. Vaughan, Patrick
226.3052

ISBN 0–7459–1440–3

Library of Congress Cataloging-in-Publication Data
Bible. N.T. Mark. English. New International. 1990.
 The Gospel of Mark illuminated/[illustrated by] Rex Nicholls:
 [notes by] Patrick Vaughan.—1st ed.
 Includes bibliographical references.
 ISBN 0–7459–1440–3
 1. Bible. N.T. Mark—Illustrations.   I. Nicholls, Rex.
II. Vaughan, Patrick, 1938–   III. Title.
BS25831990   90–33118
226.3'5208—dc20   CIP

Printed and bound in Spain

We are indebted to a number of people who assisted in different ways in preparing this book. Dr John Muddiman of Nottingham University offered many constructive remarks on a draft of the commentary notes; Dr Rami Arav of Haifa University and Mendel Nun of Kibbutz Ein Gev kindly answered correspondence about archaeology in Galilee; Louise Lancaster advised on Roman pottery designs; Christine Nicholls supplied all the scientific data on the flora and fauna; Jill Robson sparked ideas relating the imagery of text and artwork; Andrew Woodsford brought recently published archaeological material to our attention; and between them Rosemary Milner, Elsbeth Robson, Angela Tilby, Hilary Vaughan and Joanna Vaughan each made contributions towards the accuracy and intelligibility of the text. We wish to acknowledge our gratitude to each of them.

The following books were invaluable in preparing the notes and the illustrations. Those marked with an asterisk contain photographs or artwork which helped Rex Nicholls in planning particular illustrations:

J.Backhouse, *The Lindisfarne Gospels*, Phaidon, 1981

G.S.Cansdale, *Animals of Bible Lands*, Paternoster, 1970

J.H.Charlesworth, *Jesus within Judaism: New Light from Exciting Archaeological Discoveries*, SPCK, 1988

S.Corbett, 'Some Observations on the Gateways to the Herodian Temple in Jerusalem', Palestine Exploration Quarterly, vol. 84, 1952

H.Danby (trans.), *The Mishnah*, Oxford, 1933

J.Finegan, *The Archaeology of the New Testament*, Princeton, 1969

* *Great People of the Bible and How They Lived*, Readers Digest, 1974

N.Haas, 'Anthropological Observations on the Skeletal Remains from Giv'at ha-Mivtar', Israel Exploration Journal, vol. 20, 1970

N.Hareuveni, *Nature in our Biblical Heritage*, Neot Kedumim, 1980

H.St.J.Hart, 'The Crown of Thorns in John 19,2-5', Journal of Theological Studies, N.S. vol. 3, 1952

M.Hengel, *Crucifixion*, SCM, 1977

F.J.A.Hort, 'A Note by the Late Dr Hort on the Words *kophinos, spuris, sargane*', Journal of Theological Studies, vol. 10, 1909

Illustrated Bible Dictionary (3 vols), Inter Varsity Press, 1980

J.Jeremias, *The Eucharistic Words of Jesus*, SCM, 1966

* *Jerusalem Revealed*, The Israel Exploration Society, 1975

* *The Lion Encyclopedia of the Bible*, revised edition, 1986

* *The Lion Handbook to the Bible*, revised edition, 1983

* S.Loffreda, *A Visit to Capharnaum*, Franciscan Press, Jerusalem, 2nd edition, 1977

* M.Mazar, 'Herodian Jerusalem in the Light of the Excavations South and South-West of the Temple Mount', Israel Exploration Journal, vol. 28, 1978

E.M.Meyers and J.F.Strange, *Archaeology, the Rabbis and Early Christianity*, SCM, 1981

A.Millard, *Treasures from Bible Times*, Lion Publishing, 1985

* *The Model of Ancient Jerusalem at the Time of the Second Temple: Pictorial Guide*, Holyland Corp.

V.Moller-Christensen, 'Skeletal Remains from Giv'at ha-Mivtar', Israel Exploration Journal, vol. 26, 1976

J.Murphy-O'Connor, *The Holy Land: An Archaeological Guide from the Earliest Times to 1700*, Oxford, 1980

J.Naveh, 'Ossuary Inscriptions from Giv'at ha-Mivtar', Israel Exploration Journal, vol. 20, 1970

D.E.Nineham, *Saint Mark*, Penguin, 1963, the book on which Rex Nicholls' first assignment on Mark was based

M.Nun, *Ancient Anchorages and Harbours around the Sea of Galilee*, Kinnereth Sailing Co., 1988

* *Picture Archive of the Bible*, Lion Publishing, 1987

A.Raban, 'The boat from Migdal Nunia and the anchorages of the Sea of Galilee from the time of Jesus', International Journal of Nautical Archaeology and Underwater Exploration, vol. 17, 1988

H.Shanks, *Judaism in Stone: The Archaeology of Ancient Synagogues*, Harper & Row, 1979

The Story of the Bible, 2 vols, Fleetway House

C.H.V.Sutherland, *Roman Coins*, Barrie & Jenkins, 1974

V.Taylor, *The Gospel according to St Mark*, Macmillan, 1953

S.Wachsmann, 'The Galilee Boat: 2,000-year-old Hull Recovered Intact', Biblical Archaeology Review, vol. 14, no.5, Sept/Oct 1988

S.Wachsmann et al., *An Ancient Boat Discovered in the Sea of Galilee*, Israel Department of Antiquities and Museums, 1988

* J.Wilkinson, *Jerusalem as Jesus Knew It: Archaeology as Evidence*, Thames & Hudson, 1978

G.A.Williamson (trans.), *Josephus: The Jewish War*, Penguin, revised edition, 1981

Y.Yadin, 'Epigraphy and Crucifixion', Israel Exploration Journal, vol. 23, 1973

M.Zohary, *Plants of the Bible*, Cambridge, 1982

THE GOSPEL OF MARK

ILLUMINATED

Rex Nicholls

Patrick Vaughan

The Scheme of Mark's Gospel

CHAPTER ONE

Verse 1	The title of the book
2 to 8	John the Baptist prepares the way
9 to 11	Jesus is baptised
12 to 13	Jesus' temptation
14 to 15	Jesus' teaching about the kingdom of God
16 to 20	The first disciples are called
21 to 28	An evil spirit is expelled
29 to 34	Healings
35 to 39	Jesus praying and preaching
40 to 45	Leprosy healed

CHAPTER TWO

1 to 12	Paralysis healed; a dispute over authority
13 to 17	Levi called; a dispute over sinners
18 to 22	A dispute over fasting
23 to 28	A dispute over Sabbath

CHAPTER THREE

1 to 6	A dispute over healing on the Sabbath
7 to 12	Crowds follow Jesus
13 to 19	The Twelve appointed
20 to 35	A dispute over Satan

CHAPTER FOUR

1 to 9	The parable of the sower
10 to 20	Interpretation of the parables
21 to 29	More about parables
30 to 34	The parable of the mustard seed
35 to 41	Jesus rebukes a storm

CHAPTER FIVE

1 to 13	A demon-possessed man is healed
14 to 20	Gentile Decapolis hears of Jesus
21 to 34	A woman is healed
35 to 43	A dead girl is restored to life

CHAPTER SIX

1 to 6	In his home town; a prophet without honour
6 to 13	The Twelve sent out on a preaching tour
14 to 20	King Herod's fear of Jesus
21 to 29	John the Baptist is beheaded
30 to 34	Jesus seeks solitude with his disciples
35 to 44	Five thousand people are fed
45 to 65	The disciples cross the lake in safety

CHAPTER SEVEN

1 to 13	The word of God and the traditions of men
14 to 23	Clean and unclean
24 to 30	A Greek woman's faith
31 to 37	Another healing in Gentile territory

CHAPTER EIGHT

1 to 10	Four thousand people are fed
11 to 13	Seeking a sign from heaven
14 to 21	The blindness of the disciples
22 to 26	A blind man is healed by stages
27 to 33	Jesus predicts his suffering
34 to 38	Jesus' followers must expect to suffer

CHAPTER NINE

1 to 8	Jesus is transfigured
9 to 13	More teaching about the Son of Man
14 to 29	A spirit is cast out of a boy taken for dead
30 to 32	A second prediction of Jesus' suffering
33 to 41	Who is the greatest?
42 to 45	Causing little ones to stumble

CHAPTER TEN

1 to 16	Jesus teaches the dignity of women and children
17 to 23	A rich man fails to follow
24 to 31	'How hard it is to enter the kingdom of God'
32 to 45	James and John request seats of honour
46 to 52	Blind Bartimaeus receives his sight

CHAPTER ELEVEN

1 to 11	Jesus enters Jerusalem to popular acclamation
12 to 14	Jesus curses a fig-tree near Jerusalem
15 to 19	Jesus drives merchants from the Temple
20 to 26	The fig-tree and the Temple
27 to 33	Jesus' authority is challenged in the Temple

CHAPTER TWELVE

1 to 12	The parable of the vineyard and the tenants
13 to 17	Pharisees question Jesus about paying Roman poll-tax
18 to 27	Sadducees question Jesus about resurrection
28 to 34	A teacher questions Jesus about the greatest commandment
35 to 40	Jesus criticises teachers of the law
41 to 44	A poor widow offers her last penny

CHAPTER THIRTEEN

1 to 4	Jesus prophecies the Temple's destruction
5 to 13	The Last Days: a warning of the miseries preceding them
14 to 23	The Last Days: the sign for knowing their arrival
24 to 27	The Last Days: the closing scene
28 to 37	Various sayings on watchfulness

CHAPTER FOURTEEN

1 to 11	The Passion Narrative begins
12 to 16	Preparations for the Passover meal
17 to 25	The Last Supper
26 to 31	Jesus foretells the disciples' desertion and Peter's denial
32 to 42	Jesus prays in Gethsemane
43 to 51	Jesus is arrested
53 to 65	Jesus on trial before the high priest
66 to 72	Peter denies knowing Jesus

CHAPTER FIFTEEN

1 to 15	Jesus on trial before Roman authorities
16 to 20	Jesus is mistreated as a mock king
21 to 32	Jesus is crucified
33 to 41	The death of Jesus
42 to 47	The burial of Jesus

CHAPTER SIXTEEN

1 to 8	Three women visit the tomb

Contents

The Story of this Book

Original ideas, like wind-blown seeds, may germinate and take root by a series of random chance occurrences. The idea for this book took root in one original mind by such a series of chances. Here is the story.

As a graphic artist, Rex Nicholls had for years earned his livelihood through design work for the advertising, print and book trades. But personal growth seemed as important as developing his artistic skills, and in 1979 Rex took the unusual step of embarking on a part-time theology course at his local university.

One component of this course required a detailed study of Mark's Gospel. I was his tutor. Rex recalls the assignment I set for the first week's home study: 'Read straight through the Gospel text, if possible at a single sitting'. He vividly remembers the sense of astonishment which gripped him — 'the figure of Jesus stood out for me as extraordinary, and very strange'. Later he read the text again with the aid of a commentary, and once more his reading produced startling effects upon him: 'I had never realized how heavily Mark's Gospel had been influenced by Old Testament Jewish scriptures'. And so the exploration of the Jewishness of the Gospel became a special interest for Rex.

Not surprisingly, therefore, when I proposed leading a pilgrimage party to Israel in 1983, Rex and his wife Christine were amongst the first to sign up. Into that fortnight were packed a host of evocative experiences, which (unknown to us at the time) were to become a kind of resource in memory and emotion for the production of this book. Like many before him, Rex discovered that the Gospel texts had a context of geography and history, of climate and culture. By physically entering these very contexts, we learned hidden things about the Gospel story. A few incidents from our travels may make the point.

We stayed in a pilgrims' hostel within the walls of the Old City of Jerusalem. One bright morning we took a bus to the top of the Mount of Olives, just outside the city, in order to catch something of the experience of Jesus' arrival at that point as that last fateful week began. As he topped the brow of the hill, the city came in sight, and being deeply moved, he wept over it. So we too slowly walked down the lane from the summit, astonished at the beautiful sight of the city across the valley, and the glistening golden Dome of the Rock on the very spot where once the ancient Temple stood. Then, next day (a Thursday) another memorable walk after supper. Taking torches in hand, we walked silently through the narrow city alleys, out of the Dung Gate; turning off the main road, we found a track down the steep slope to the Kidron stream, and crossing it, came to Gethsemane and an olive grove. Never was solitude beneath a tree more moving, nor the battlemented walls of the city above more menacing.

Shared experiences such as these etch their way into memory, so that years later, whenever a Gospel text is read, the mind's eye readily supplies a context. With Rex's drawing skills, it was natural that he should one day desire to give actual visible form to his reflections.

Some time later we went on a pilgrimage of a different kind, to Holy Island, just off the coast of north-east England, known in earlier times as Lindisfarne. Our party stayed for several days on Lindisfarne itself, soaking in the atmosphere and the history.

Inevitably the extraordinary story of Cuthbert, bishop of Lindisfarne, who died there in 687, became a focus of our interest. Cuthbert's story is extraordinary not so much for what he did during his holy life, but for what happened to him after death. Universally recognized in life as a holy man, Cuthbert was buried within the church of the monastery on Lindisfarne — the centre from which northern Britain had been evangelized. Eleven years later the monks, believing that the relics of a potential saint rested beneath the floor, opened Cuthbert's grave, and to their delight discovered that the body had not corrupted — a miraculous sign that Cuthbert was indeed a saint. The body was reverently placed in a casket and laid on the floor of the church sanctuary: pilgrims flocked to the shrine.

To celebrate this great event, Eadfrith, Cuthbert's successor as bishop, undertook a task of devoted craftsmanship. With his own hand, he produced a glorious illuminated book of the latin text of the four Gospels, all apparently achieved within the space of two years. The truly astonishing thing about this book (now called the Lindisfarne Gospels) is that it has survived virtually intact down into our own times, over 1,200 years later.

An abiding memory of our stay on Holy Island is the morning on which I was loaned the key to the locked display case in the parish church, where a facsimile copy of the great Gospel-book is exhibited. Opening the case, we were able to turn over the pages at leisure, marvelling at the intricacy of geometric design, the beauty of colour and the sheer daring of some of the calligraphy. Turning to the very last page, we found the paragraph written in Latin by a later scribe:

'Eadfrith, Bishop of Lindisfarne, originally wrote this book, for God and for Saint Cuthbert and — jointly — for all the saints whose relics are in the Island. And Ethelwald, bishop of the Lindisfarne islanders, impressed it on the outside and covered it — as he well knew how to do. And Billfrith, the anchorite, forged the ornaments which are on it on the outside and adorned it with gold and with gems and also with gilded-over silver — pure metal . . .

On the way home, we stopped at Durham Cathedral, where Cuthbert's remains were finally laid to rest after a century of being carried around: for when it had become impossible to live safely on Lindisfarne because of Viking attacks from across the sea, the community of monks evacuated to the mainland, taking with them Cuthbert's coffin and several other treasures, amongst them the great Gospel-book. By kind arrangement with the Cathedral Librarian we were taken to the stone-vaulted manuscript room. Steadily before our astonished eyes he took down from their shelves some of the Cathedral's special manuscript treasures, including fragments of Gospel-books written in Northumbria in the seventh and eighth centuries. The pages were well worn with use, and the designs faded or damaged, but the sense was quite overpowering of being in touch with artists of great antiquity. For there on the table in front of us lay their books, whose vellum pages we could turn over with due care and reverence.

We learned that during the seventh and eighth centuries the Anglo-Saxon kingdom of Northumbria had been a great centre for the production and export of books, especially at the newly-founded monasteries of Jarrow, Monkwearmouth and Lindisfarne. A very distinctive style of illuminated Gospel-books had developed in which the Celtic tradition of elaborate interlace patterns were a notable feature. A surprising number produced in this style still survive. Some may be seen in the cathedral libraries of Durham, Lichfield and Hereford. Similar Northumbrian Gospel-books are also to be seen in several European libraries, including Paris, Leipzig, Maeseyck, Trier, Stuttgart, Leningrad and St Gall.

The Lindisfarne Gospels, however, are not now in Durham. When the monastery was dissolved by King Henry VIII in 1539, its treasures were seized by the Crown and taken to London. The great Gospel-book must have been amongst the items seized. Eventually it found its way to the British Library where it is on permanent public display. So to the British Library our trail was bound to lead.

We found ourselves there during another student expedition, this time exploring treasures from the biblical and Christian past in the British Museum. After visiting the galleries with monumental carved stone reliefs and rooms with early Christian silver treasure hoards, we came to the manuscript room of the British Library. Its rows of glass-topped cases by comparison with the archaeological treasures looked boringly similar. But gathering round the case containing the Lindisfarne Gospels, we became aware that we were looking at one of the earliest surviving examples of a book written and made in Britain. The light was dim (for reasons of conservation) and only a single opening was on display. But we had seen it.

Rex lingered there after the rest of us had moved on. In those few moments, a seed was sown which has germinated and years later borne fruit in this present book.

THE ARTIST AND THE GOSPEL

This book has the feel of an illuminated manuscript. Each page holds at its centre a paragraph from the text of Mark's Gospel, scripted by Bob Bond. In smaller type in the margins appear passages from the Jewish scriptures to which Mark's text may be making allusion. Occasionally the margins also include quotations from non-scriptural contemporary writings. Rex Nicholls' coloured drawings set the atmosphere for the page's text.

The book is the fruit of Rex's personal reflections on the text of Mark's Gospel, in the light of what he has seen with the eye on pilgrimage and with the imagination in meditation.

The overall intention is to offer to the modern reader something of the feel of how Mark's text might have been heard and understood by its first readers. The very earliest Christians were all Jews. Even as the church spread to Greek-speaking cities around the eastern Mediterranean, the first contact a Christian evangelist would try to make would be with the Jewish synagogue.

Jewish culture has always been an extremely literate one. The central ritual of synagogue worship consisted of reading from the scrolls of the Law and the Prophets. Every adult man was expected to be capable of doing this. Private study of these texts, and meditation on them, was an important aspect of Jewish devotion. As a result, many people knew large portions of the scriptures off by heart and scriptural allusions were a common part of everyday conversation.

It is hardly surprising, therefore, that in preaching their message about Jesus, the earliest Christian evangelists made frequent allusion to these Jewish scriptures (which today are commonly called the Old Testament). So when it came to writing down the Gospel story, the same process continued. Sometimes the source of a quotation is declared in the text (as in the second verse of Mark's Gospel). But much more often it is a matter of tacit allusion (as, for instance, when stories of Jesus appear to parallel those of the ancient prophets Moses and Elijah). There was a presumption that the original readers would catch the allusion. Unfortunately these kind of allusions are completely lost on modern readers who are unfamiliar with the Old Testament.

The quotations written in smaller type in the margins bring onto the page the kinds of allusion which the first readers might instinctively have picked up. What was then implicit is here made explicit, so that at a glance the modern reader may enjoy picking up the resonances of the Gospel text.

The drawings on each page provide visual 'sidelights', bringing new things into view. The drawings are not illustrations, in the usual sense. Rather, they supply an atmosphere of visual allusion which illuminates (as distinct from illustrates) the meaning. Often the design of a page is symbolic; though sometimes it offers historical or geographical material. In every case, the finished page invites the enquiring eye to explore. Perhaps it will be the meticulous detail of the artist's craft which attracts the eye, or the general design of a page, or the relationship between blocks of text and the drawings. Whether the eye slowly wanders round the page or stays with a particular feature, what it sees will stimulate the imagination, which in turn may lead to a pondering on the meaning of the central text. In this way a pattern of relaxed meditation may be set up.

FOR FURTHER REFLECTION

For those readers who may appreciate analytical or background comments on the contents of each page, detailed notes have been supplied at the end of the book, on pages 101 to 128. These notes are arranged with one column to every full colour page. Three categories of comments are offered: on the visual design of the page layout as a whole; on the meaning of that paragraph of Mark's text; and on technical details of geography, history, flora, fauna, and so on. A marker kept in this part of the book will facilitate easy cross-reference between each coloured page and the relevant column of notes.

Some readers may be curious about the writer of this Gospel. What can be known about him? What were his intentions? How did he collect his material? What principles guided his arrangement of it? These and other questions about the composition of the Gospel are discussed on pages 97 to 100.

One general aspect of the artist's strategy is worth commenting on here. Readers will quickly notice a surprising absence: people hardly appear. In this respect the book is quite unlike most illustrated Bibles. Rex deliberately decided not to depict the figure of Jesus at all. The reason is not far to seek. In historical reality, Jesus was a Jew with semitic features, about thirty years old. But every person who has ever heard of Jesus has already constructed in their imagination some impression of what they think he looks like. It follows that any artist's impression of Jesus will shatter the personal images already built up in readers' imaginations; and hinder their meditational use of the book. Once this policy had been decided, the exclusion of all other human figures seemed a logical consequence. The lack of human representation gives readers the opportunity of peopling the pages in their own way, as their imagination leads them.

The whole book reveals how the text of the earliest Gospel has come alive in Rex Nicholls' imagination, making its ancient words shine out with remarkable clarity through this 'illuminated Gospel'.

Patrick Vaughan

page 11
The evangelist

A wide-eyed figure, drawn in a very stylized manner, is seated at a writing desk. It is the evangelist, preparing to write the opening words of his book. He looks up at the reader—with an expression which suggests that he is lost in wonderment at the story he is about to tell. Above him is a winged lion, holding a book in its paw and a trumpet in its mouth. This strange creature is the traditional symbol for Mark and his Gospel. It looks as though the lion is blowing a fanfare to accompany the reading of the opening words.

This page is unlike any other in the book: it bears a representation of the human figure. But the figure is no one in the story: it is the story's compiler. In placing a picture of the evangelist here, Rex Nicholls is following a tradition of illuminated gospel-books: before the text of each Gospel began, it was common to include a full-page illustration of the evangelist and his symbol. It was a pictorial way of making a theological claim: the words which followed were thought of as divinely inspired (mediated to the evangelist by the symbolic creature), even though they were the creation of a human mind.

The lion as a traditional symbol for Mark's Gospel is derived from the vision of the heavenly court described in Revelation 4: 'In the centre, around the throne, were four living creatures . . . The first creature was like a lion, the second was like an ox, the third had a face like a man, the fourth was like a flying eagle'. As Christian art developed, these creatures came to be regarded as the symbols of the Gospels of Mark, Luke, Matthew and John, respectively.

In designing this page, Rex Nicholls has been influenced by one particular page in the Lindisfarne Gospels (folio 93b). He has followed the stylised painting of Bishop Eadfrith, but he has added the modern tools of his trade—coloured lead pencils, a surgical scalpel and an eraser.

page 12
CHAPTER 1:1

The title of the book

The first sentence of the book is really its title. Like any well chosen book title, it quickly gives an impression of the contents. Three points are made by the title. First, the writing which follows is 'gospel', meaning 'good news'; second, it is about someone called Jesus Christ; and third, this person is here described as 'Son of God'.

At the time when these words were first written, no one thought of 'the gospel' as a book. 'Gospel' was a technical word used by the first Christians in a very specialized sense. By this word, they meant a list of facts about Jesus, together with claims about their meaning, which were commonly recited in any public explanation of their faith. To judge from the speeches given in the Acts of the Apostles, the list of things which needed to be mentioned in explaining the Christian faith included the following: (1) after John the Baptist had been active, Jesus of Nazareth came on the scene; (2) he went about doing good works and healing; (3) but the people of Jerusalem and their leaders asked Pilate to have him executed; (4) he was executed by crucifixion and then buried; (5) but God raised him up; (6) and we who speak to you are witnesses of these things; (7) they have all happened in accordance with prophecies in the ancient scriptures; (8) so turn to God, be baptised in the name of Jesus, for he is the Christ, the one who is to be the judge of the world.

The first Christians fastened on the Greek word *euangelion* to describe this list. In ordinary Greek this word meant 'a message of good news', and that was precisely what the first Christians considered this information about Jesus to be. It is no coincidence that the contents of this book more or less correspond with the items in the list of things to be mentioned in explaining Christian faith.

So by giving his book this title, the evangelist was indicating to Christians that he was about to put in writing a particular message which, up to this point, had always been communicated by word of mouth. He could not have guessed that he was pioneering a new genre of literature which would later be called 'gospels'.

To Christine

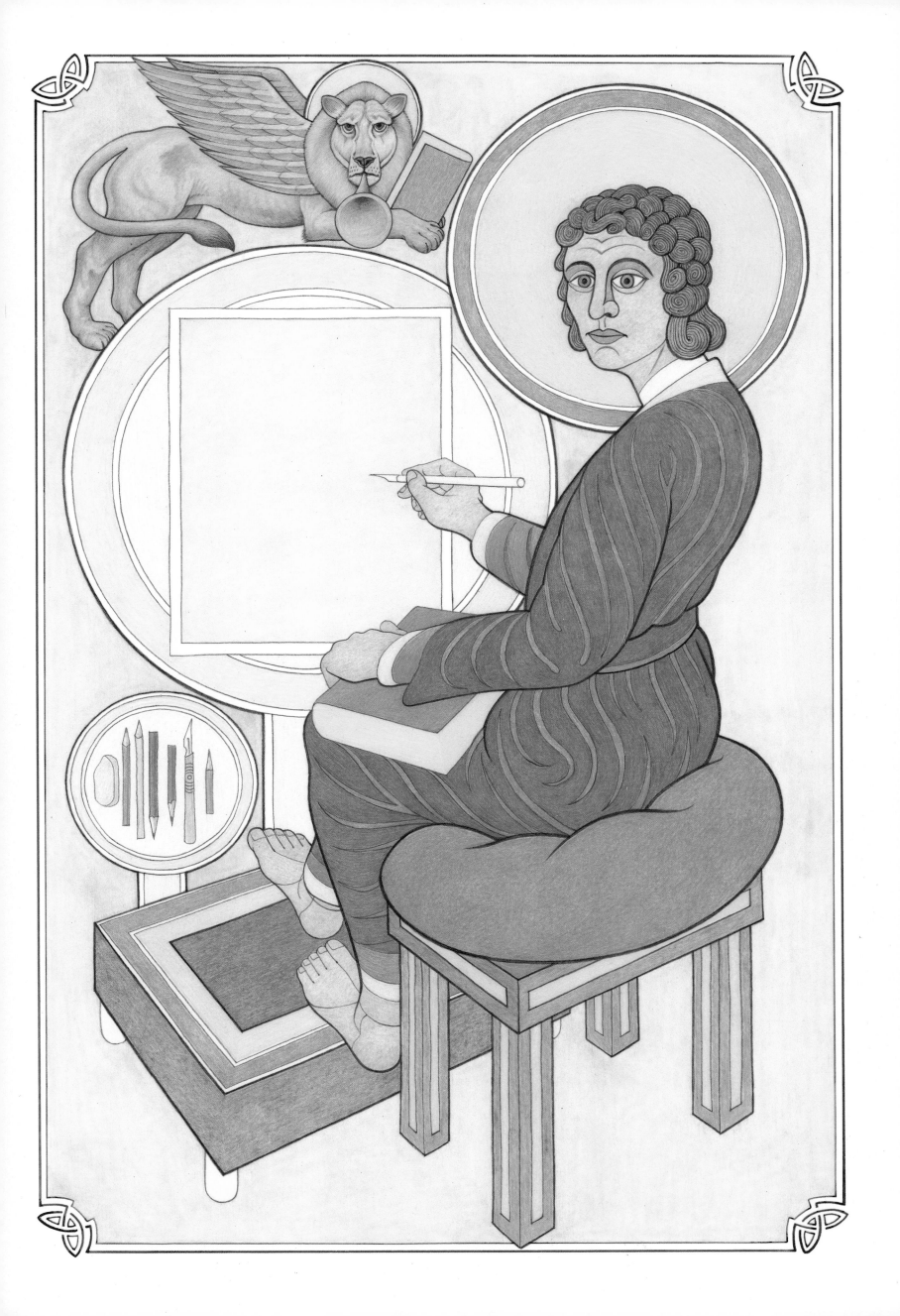

The
beginning
of the gospel
about
Jesus Christ,
the Son of
God...

It is written in Isaiah the prophet:
"I will send my messenger ahead of you, who will prepare your way"—
"a voice of one calling in the desert, 'Prepare the way for the Lord, make straight paths for him.'"
And so John came, baptising in the desert region and preaching a baptism of repentance for the forgiveness of sins. The whole Judean countryside and all the people of Jerusalem went out to him. Confessing their sins, they were baptised by him in the Jordan River. John wore clothing made of camel's hair, with a leather belt round his waist, and he ate locusts and wild honey. And this was his message: "After me will come one more powerful than I, the thong of whose sandals I am not worthy to stoop down and untie. I baptise you with water, but he will baptise you with the Holy Spirit."

At that time Jesus came from Nazareth in Galilee and was baptised by John in the Jordan. As Jesus was coming up out of the water, he saw heaven being torn open and the Spirit descending on him like a dove. And a voice came from heaven: "You are my Son, whom I love; with you I am well pleased."

THE PROMISED SERVANT

Isaiah 42:1

"Here is my servant whom I uphold, my chosen one in whom I delight; I will put my Spirit on him and he will bring justice to the nations."

THE PROMISED SON

Psalm 2:7–8

I will proclaim the decree of the Lord: He said to me,
"You are my Son; today I have become your Father. Ask of me, and I will make the nations your inheritance, the ends of the earth your possession."

VISIONS OF HUMANITY AT PEACE WITH NATURE

Isaiah 11:6–9

The wolf will live with the lamb, the leopard will lie down with the goat, the calf and the lion and the yearling together; and a little child will lead them. The cow will feed with the bear, their young will lie down together, and the lion will eat straw like the ox. The infant will play near the hole of the cobra, and the young child put his hand into the viper's nest. They will neither harm nor destroy on all my holy mountain.

Hosea 2:18

In that day I will make a covenant for them with the beasts of the field and the birds of the air and the creatures that move along the ground. Bow and sword and battle I will abolish from the land, so that all may lie down in safety.

Psalm 91:11–14

For he will command his angels concerning you to guard you in all your ways; they will lift you up in their hands, so that you will not strike your foot against a stone. You will tread upon the lion and the cobra; you will trample the great lion and the serpent. "Because he loves me," says the Lord, "I will rescue him; I will protect him, for he acknowledges my name."

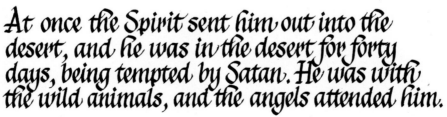

At once the Spirit sent him out into the desert, and he was in the desert for forty days, being tempted by Satan. He was with the wild animals, and the angels attended him.

ELIJAH IN THE DESERT

1 Kings 19:5–8

Then he lay down under the tree and fell asleep. All at once an angel touched him and said, "Get up and eat." He looked around, and there by his head was a cake of bread baked over hot coals, and a jar of water. He ate and drank and then lay down again. The angel of the Lord came back a second time and touched him and said, "Get up and eat, for the journey is too much for you." So he got up and ate and drank. Strengthened by that food, he travelled for forty days and forty nights until he reached Horeb, the mountain of God.

MOSES IN THE DESERT

Exodus 15:22,24

Then Moses led Israel from the Red Sea and they went into the Desert of Shur. For three days they travelled in the desert without finding water. So the people grumbled against Moses, saying, "What are we to drink?"

Exodus 24:18

Then Moses entered the cloud as he went on up the mountain. And he stayed on the mountain forty days and forty nights.

After John was put in prison
Jesus went into Galilee
proclaiming the Gospel of God.

"The time has come,
the kingdom of
God is near. Repent
and believe the
good news!"

GOSPEL: GOOD NEWS

Isaiah 40:9

You who bring good tidings to Zion, go up on a high mountain. You who bring good tidings to Jerusalem, lift up your voice with a shout, lift it up, do not be afraid; say to the towns of Judah, "Here is your God!"

Isaiah 52:7

How beautiful on the mountains are the feet of those who bring good news, who proclaim peace, who bring good tidings, who proclaim salvation, who say to Zion, "Your God reigns!"

Isaiah 61:1

The Spirit of the Sovereign Lord is on me, because the Lord has anointed me to preach good news to the poor. He has sent me to bind up the broken-hearted, to proclaim freedom for the captives and recovery of sight for the blind.

'REPENT'

Psalm 51:10,17

Create in me a pure heart, O God, and renew a steadfast spirit within me . . . The sacrifices of God are a broken spirit; a broken and contrite heart, O God, you will not despise.

Joel 2:12–13

"Even now," declares the Lord, "return to me with all your heart, with fasting and weeping and mourning. Rend your heart and not your garments." Return to the Lord your God, for he is gracious and compassionate, slow to anger and abounding in love, and he relents from sending calamity.

'THE TIME HAS COME'

Daniel 12:4

But you, Daniel, close up and seal the words of the scroll until the time of the end.

Ezekiel 7:2–3,12

"Son of man, this is what the Sovereign Lord says to the land of Israel: The end! The end has come upon the four corners of the land. The end is now upon you and I will unleash my anger against you. I will judge you according to your conduct and repay you for all your detestable practices . . . The time has come, the day has arrived."

As Jesus walked beside the Sea of Galilee, he saw Simon and his brother Andrew casting a net into the lake, for they were fishermen. "Come, follow me," Jesus said, "and I will make you fishers of men." At once they left their nets and followed him. When he had gone a little farther, he saw James son of Zebedee and his brother John in a boat, preparing their nets. Without delay he called them, and they left their father Zebedee in the boat with the hired men and followed him.

THE PROPHET ELISHA'S CALL

1 Kings 19:19–21

So Elijah went from there and found Elisha son of Shaphat. He was ploughing with twelve yoke of oxen, and he himself was driving the twelfth pair. Elijah went up to him and threw his cloak around him. Elisha then left his oxen and ran after Elijah. "Let me kiss my father and mother good-bye," he said, "and then I will come with you." "Go back," Elijah replied. "What have I done to you?" So Elisha left him and went back. He took his yoke of oxen and slaughtered them. He burned the ploughing equipment to cook the meat and gave it to the people, and they ate. Then he set out to follow Elijah and became his attendant.

'FISHERS OF MEN'

Habakkuk 1:14

You have made men like fish in the sea, like sea creatures that have no ruler.

Jeremiah 16:16

"But now I will send for many fishermen," declares the Lord, "and they will catch them."

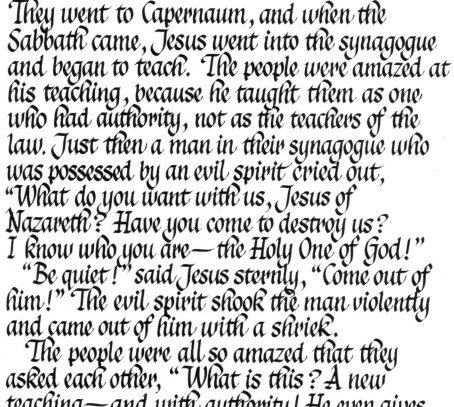

They went to Capernaum, and when the Sabbath came, Jesus went into the synagogue and began to teach. The people were amazed at his teaching, because he taught them as one who had authority, not as the teachers of the law. Just then a man in their synagogue who was possessed by an evil spirit cried out, "What do you want with us, Jesus of Nazareth? Have you come to destroy us? I know who you are—the Holy One of God!"

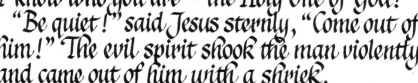
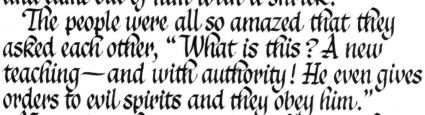

"Be quiet!" said Jesus sternly, "Come out of him!" The evil spirit shook the man violently and came out of him with a shriek.

The people were all so amazed that they asked each other, "What is this? A new teaching—and with authority! He even gives orders to evil spirits and they obey him."

News about him spread quickly over the whole region of Galilee.

'THE HOLY ONE OF GOD!'

Psalm 16:10

You will not abandon me to the grave, nor will you let your Holy One see decay.

SIGNS OF GOD'S REDEMPTION

Exodus 15:26

The Lord said, "If you listen carefully to the voice of the Lord your God and do what is right in his eyes, if you pay attention to his commands and keep all his decrees, I will not bring on you any of the diseases I brought on the Egyptians, for I am the Lord, who heals you."

'BALM IN GILEAD'

Jeremiah 8:22

Is there no balm in Gilead? Is there no physician there? Why then is there no healing for the wound of my people?

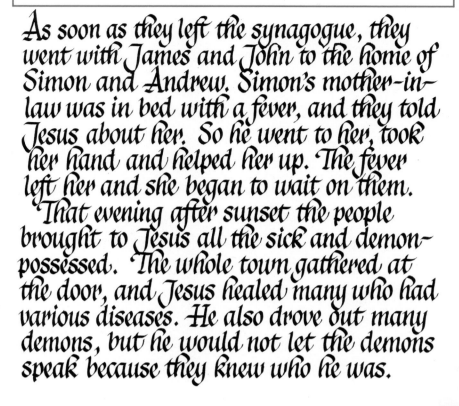

As soon as they left the synagogue, they went with James and John to the home of Simon and Andrew. Simon's mother-in-law was in bed with a fever, and they told Jesus about her. So he went to her, took her hand and helped her up. The fever left her and she began to wait on them. That evening after sunset the people brought to Jesus all the sick and demon-possessed. The whole town gathered at the door, and Jesus healed many who had various diseases. He also drove out many demons, but he would not let the demons speak because they knew who he was.

HEALING

Malachi 4:2

But for you who revere my name, the sun of righteousness will rise with healing in its wings. And you will go out and leap like calves released from the stall.

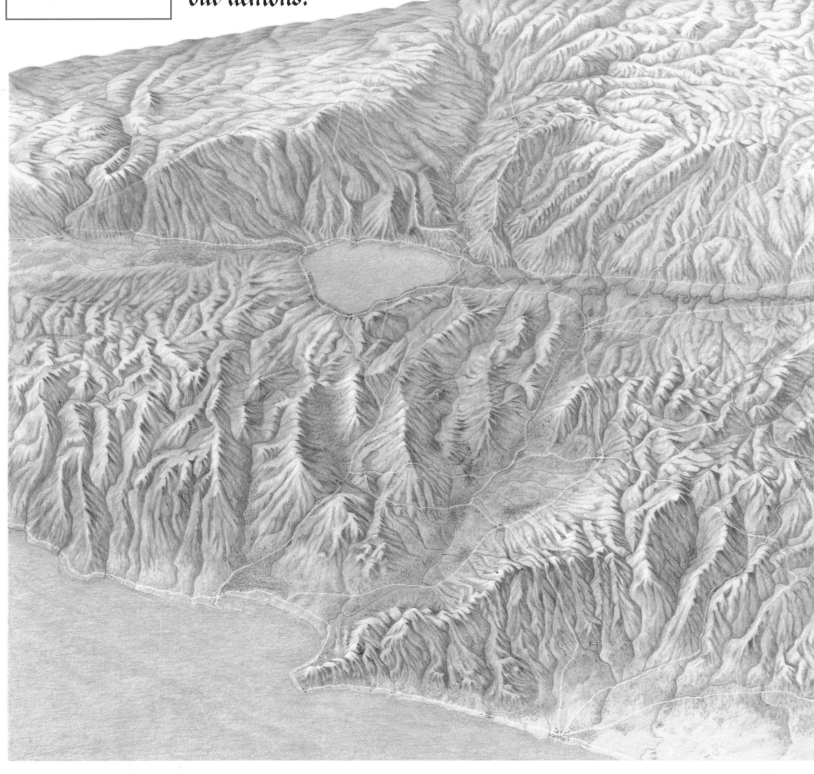

'VERY EARLY IN THE MORNING'

Psalm 5:3

Morning by morning, O Lord, you hear my voice; morning by morning I lay my requests before you and wait in expectation.

Psalm 88:13

But I cry to you for help, O Lord; in the morning my prayer comes before you.

Psalm 119:147

I rise before dawn and cry for help; I have put my hope in your word.

Very early in the morning, while it was still dark, Jesus got up, left the house and went off to a solitary place, where he prayed. Simon and his companions went to look for him, and when they found him, they exclaimed: "Everyone is looking for you!" Jesus replied, "Let us go somewhere else—to the nearby villages—so that I can preach there also. That is why I have come." So he travelled throughout Galilee, preaching in their synagogues and driving out demons.

RITUALS FOR CLEANSING LEPROSY

Leviticus 14:1–11, 19–20

The Lord said to Moses, ''These are the regulations for the diseased person at the time of his ceremonial cleansing, when he is brought to the priest. The priest is to go outside the camp and examine him. If the person has been healed of his infectious skin disease, the priest shall order that two live clean birds and some cedar wood, scarlet yarn and hyssop be brought for the one to be cleansed. Then the priest shall order that one of the birds be killed over fresh water in a clay pot. He is then to take the live bird and dip it. together with the cedar wood, the scarlet yarn and the hyssop, into the blood of the bird that was killed over the fresh water. Seven times he shall sprinkle the one to be cleansed of the infectious disease and pronounce him clean. Then he is to release the live bird in the open fields. The person to be cleansed must wash his clothes, shave off all his hair and bathe with water; then he will be ceremonially clean. After this he may come into the camp, but he must stay outside his tent for seven days. On the seventh day he must shave off all his hair; he must shave his head, his beard, his eyebrows and

A man with leprosy came to him and begged him on his knees, "If you are willing you can make me clean." Filled with compassion, Jesus reached out his hand and touched the man. "I am willing," he said. "Be clean!" Immediately the leprosy left him and he was cured. Jesus sent him away at once with a strong warning: "See that you don't tell this to anyone. But go, show yourself to the priest and offer the sacrifices that Moses commanded for your cleansing, as a testimony to them. Instead he went out and began to talk freely, spreading the news. As a result, Jesus could no longer enter a town openly but stayed outside in lonely places. Yet the people still came to him from everywhere.

the rest of his hair. He must wash his clothes and bathe himself with water, and he will be clean. On the eighth day he must bring two male lambs and one ewe lamb a year old, each without defect, along with three-tenths of an ephah of fine flour mixed with oil for a grain offering, and one log of oil. The priest who pronounces him clean shall present both the one to be cleansed and his offerings before the Lord at the entrance to the Tent of Meeting . . . Then the priest is to sacrifice the sin offering and make atonement for the one to be cleansed from his uncleanness. After that, the priest shall slaughter the burnt offering and offer it on the altar, together with the grain offering, and make atonement for him, and he will be clean.

2

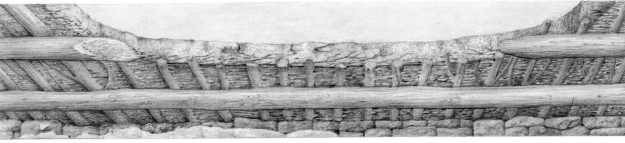

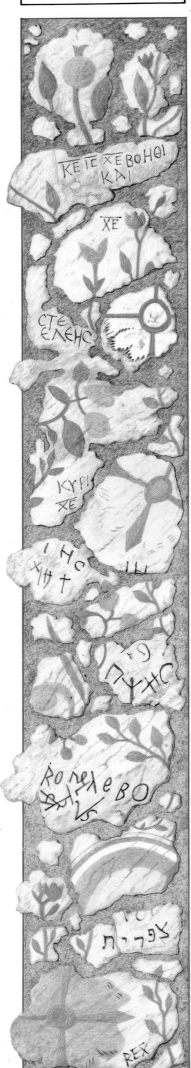

A few days later, when Jesus again entered Capernaum, the people heard that he had come home. So many gathered that there was no room left, not even outside the door, and he preached the word to them. Some men came, bringing to him a paralytic, carried by four of them. Since they could not get him to Jesus because of the crowd, they made an opening in the roof above Jesus and, after digging through it, lowered the mat the paralysed man was lying on. When Jesus saw their faith, he said to the paralytic, "Son, your sins are forgiven." Now some teachers of the law were sitting there, thinking to themselves, "Why does this fellow talk like that? He's blaspheming! Who can forgive sins but God alone?"

Immediately Jesus knew in his spirit that this was what they were thinking in their hearts, and he said to them, "Why are you thinking these things? Which is easier; to say to the paralytic, 'Your sins are forgiven,' or to say, 'Get up, take your mat and walk'? But that you may know that the Son of Man has authority on earth to forgive sins..." He said to the paralytic, "I tell you, get up, take your mat and go home." He got up, took his mat and walked out in full view of them all. This amazed everyone and they praised God, saying, "We have never seen anything like this!"

GOD'S FORGIVENESS

Psalm 103:2–3

Praise the Lord, O my soul, and forget not all his benefits. He forgives all my sins and heals all my diseases.

Psalm 130:3–4

If you, O Lord, kept a record of sins, O Lord, who could stand? But with you there is forgiveness; therefore you are feared.

'SON OF MAN'

Daniel 7:13–14

In my vision at night I looked, and there before me was one like a son of man, coming with the clouds of heaven. He approached the Ancient of Days and was led into his presence. He was given authority, glory and sovereign power; all peoples, nations and men of every language worshipped him. His dominion is an everlasting dominion that will not pass away, and his kingdom is one that will never be destroyed.

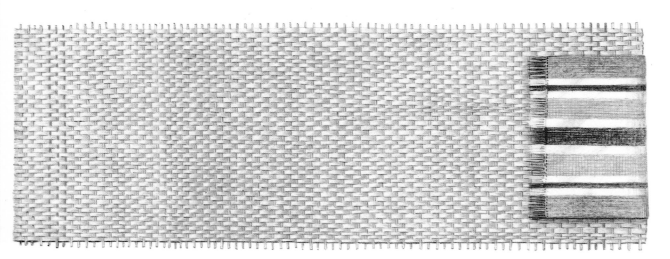

Once again Jesus went out beside the lake. A large crowd came to him, and he began to teach them. As he walked along he saw Levi son of Alphaeus sitting at the tax collector's booth. "Follow me," Jesus told him, and Levi got up and followed him. While Jesus was having dinner at Levi's house, many tax collectors and 'sinners' were eating with him and his disciples, for there were many who followed him. When the teachers of the law who were Pharisees saw him eating with the 'sinners' and tax collectors, they asked his disciples: "Why does he eat with tax collectors and 'sinners'?" On hearing this, Jesus said to them, "It is not the healthy who need a doctor, but the sick. I have not come to call the righteous, but sinners."

PHARISEES

Josephus, Antiquities 17:2,4

A certain sect who prided themselves in the exact skill they had in the law of their fathers, and made people believe they were highly favoured by God.

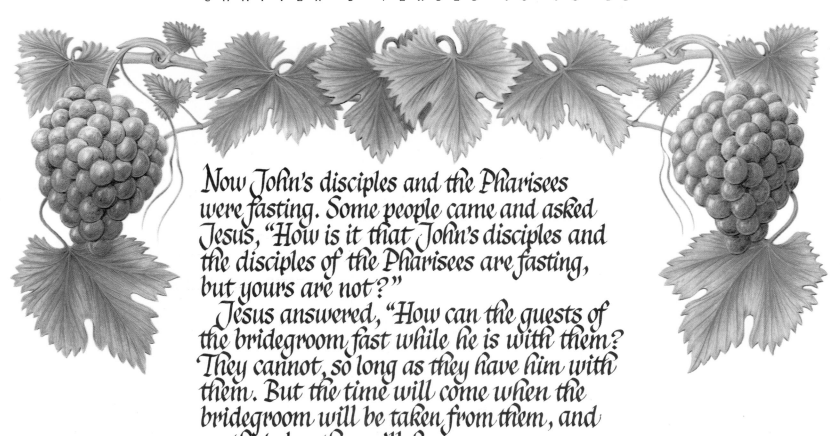

Now John's disciples and the Pharisees were fasting. Some people came and asked Jesus, "How is it that John's disciples and the disciples of the Pharisees are fasting, but yours are not?"

Jesus answered, "How can the guests of the bridegroom fast while he is with them? They cannot, so long as they have him with them. But the time will come when the bridegroom will be taken from them, and on that day they will fast.

"No-one sews a patch of unshrunk cloth on an old garment. If he does, the new piece will pull away from the old, making the tear worse. And no-one pours new wine into old wineskins. If he does, the wine will burst the skins, and both the wine and the wineskins will be ruined. No, he pours new wine into new wineskins."

Isaiah 54:5–6

"For your Maker is your husband – the Lord Almighty is his name – the Holy One of Israel, is your Redeemer; he is called the God of all the earth. The Lord will call you back as if you were a wife deserted and distressed in spirit – a wife who married young, only to be rejected," says your God.

THE BRIDEGROOM

Isaiah 62:4–5

No longer will they call you Deserted, or name your land Desolate. But you will be called Hephzibah, ('My delight is in her') and your land Beulah ('Married'), for the Lord will take delight in you, and your land will be married. As a young man marries a maiden, so will your sons marry you; as a bridegroom rejoices over his bride, so will your God rejoice over you.

Hosea 2:16, 19–20

"In that day," declares the Lord, "you will call me 'my husband'; you will no longer call me 'my master' . . . I will betroth you to me for ever; I will betroth you in righteousness and justice, in love and compassion. I will betroth you in faithfulness, and you will acknowledge the Lord."

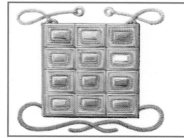

ABIATHAR BECOMES DAVID'S PRIEST   1 Samuel 22:20–23

But Abiathar, son of Ahimelech, son of Ahitub, escaped and fled to join David. He told David that Saul had killed the priests of the Lord. Then David said to Abiathar: '' . . . Stay with me; don't be afraid; the man who is seeking your life is seeking mine also. You will be safe with me.''

OBSERVANCE OF THE SABBATH

Exodus 20:8–11

''Remember the Sabbath day by keeping it holy. Six days you shall labour and do all your work, but the seventh day is a Sabbath to the Lord your God. On it you shall not do any work, neither you, nor your son or daughter, nor your manservant or maidservant, nor your animals, nor the alien within your gates. For in six days the Lord made the heavens and the earth, the sea, and all that is in them, but he rested on the seventh day. Therefore the Lord blessed the Sabbath day and made it holy.

THE HUNGRY TRAVELLER

Deuteronomy 23:25

If you enter your neighbour's cornfield, you may pick the ears with your hands, but you must not put a sickle to his standing corn.

One Sabbath Jesus was going through the cornfields, and as his disciples walked along, they began to pick some ears of corn. The Pharisees said to him, "Look, why are they doing what is unlawful on the Sabbath?"

He answered, "Have you never read what David did when he and his companions were hungry and in need? In the days of Abiathar the high priest, he entered the house of God and ate the consecrated bread, which is lawful only for priests to eat. And he also gave some to his companions."

Then he said to them, "The Sabbath was made for man, not man for the Sabbath. So the Son of Man is Lord even of the Sabbath."

DAVID AS A STARVING OUTLAW

1 Samuel 21:1–6

David went to Nob, to Ahimelech the priest. Ahimelech trembled when he met him, and asked, ''Why are you alone? Why is no-one with you?'' David answered Ahimelech the priest, ''The king charged me with a certain matter and said to me, 'No-one is to know anything about your mission and your instructions.' As for my men, I have told them to meet me at a certain place. Now then, what have you to hand? Give me five loaves of bread, or whatever you can find.'' But the priest answered David, ''I don't have any ordinary bread to hand; however, there is some consecrated bread here – provided the men have kept themselves from women,'' David replied. ''Indeed women have been kept from us, as usual whenever I set out. The men's bodies are holy even on missions that are not holy. How much more so today!'' So the priest gave him the consecrated bread, since there was no bread there except the bread of the Presence that had been removed from before the Lord and replaced by hot bread on the day it was taken away.

'THE TABLE OF PURE GOLD'

Exodus 25:23–28

Make a table of acacia wood – two cubits long, a cubit wide and a cubit and a half high. Overlay it with pure gold and make a gold moulding around it. Also make around it a rim a handbreadth wide and put a gold moulding on

THE BREAD OF THE PRESENCE   Leviticus 24:5–9

Take fine flour and bake twelve loaves of bread, using two-tenths of an ephah for each loaf. Set them in two rows, six in each row, on the table of pure gold before the Lord. Along each row put some pure incense as a memorial portion to represent the bread and to be an offering made to the Lord by fire. This bread is to be set out before the Lord regularly, Sabbath after Sabbath, on behalf of the Israelites, as a lasting covenant. It belongs to Aaron and his sons, who are to eat it in a holy place, because it is a most holy part of their regular share of the offerings made to the Lord by fire.

the rim. Make four gold rings for the table and fasten them to the four corners, where the legs are. The rings are to be close to the rim to hold the poles used in carrying the table. Make the poles of acacia wood, overlay them with gold and carry the table with them.

Another time he went into the synagogue, and a man with a shrivelled hand was there. Some of them were looking for a reason to accuse Jesus, so they watched him closely to see if he would heal him on the Sabbath. Jesus said to the man with the shrivelled hand, "Stand up in front of everyone."

Then Jesus asked them, "Which is lawful on the Sabbath: to do good or to do evil, to save life or to kill?" But they remained silent.

He looked round at them in anger and, deeply distressed at their stubborn hearts, said to the man, "Stretch out your hand." He stretched it out, and his hand was completely restored. Then the Pharisees went out and began to plot with the Herodians how they might kill Jesus.

THE SABBATH

Leviticus 23:3

There are six days when you may work, but the seventh day is a Sabbath of rest, a day of solemn assembly. You are not to do any work; wherever you live, it is a Sabbath to the Lord.

Jesus withdrew with his disciples to the lake, and a large crowd from Galilee followed. When they heard all he was doing, many people came to him from Judea, Jerusalem, Idumea, and the regions across the Jordan and around Tyre and Sidon. Because of the crowd he told his disciples to have a small boat ready for him, to keep the people from crowding him. For he had healed many, so that those with diseases were pushing forward to touch him. Whenever the evil spirits saw him, they fell down before him and cried out, "You are the Son of God." But he gave them strict orders not to tell who he was.

'SON OF GOD'

2 Samuel 7:4–5, 14

That night the word of the Lord came to Nathan, saying:
"Go and tell my servant David, 'This is what the Lord says . . . I will be his father, and he shall be my Son.'"

HYMNS USED IN THE ROYAL TEMPLE

Psalm 2:7

I will proclaim the decree of the Lord:
"You are my Son, today I have become your Father."

Psalm 89:26–27

He will call out to me, "You are my Father, my God, the Rock my Saviour." I will also appoint him my firstborn, the most exalted of the kings of the earth.

THE TWELVE TRIBES OF ISRAEL **Genesis 35:22–26**

Jacob had twelve sons:
The sons of Leah:
Reuben the firstborn of Jacob, Simeon, Levi, Judah, Issachar and Zebulun.
The sons of Rachel:
Joseph and Benjamin.
The sons of Rachel's maidservant Bilhah:
Dan and Naphtali
The sons of Leah's maidservant Zilpah:
Gad and Asher.
These were the sons of Jacob, who were born to him in Paddan Aram.

Jesus went up into the hills and called to him those he wanted, and they came to him. He appointed twelve—designating them apostles—that they might be with him and that he might send them out to preach and to have authority to drive out demons. These are the twelve he appointed: Simon (to whom he gave the name Peter); James son of Zebedee, and his brother John (to them he gave the name Boanerges, which means Sons of Thunder); Andrew, Philip, Bartholomew, Matthew, Thomas, James son of Alphaeus, Thaddaeus, Simon the Zealot and Judas Iscariot, who betrayed him.

'BEELZEBUB'

2 Kings 1:2

Now Ahaziah had fallen through the lattice of his upper room in Samaria and injured himself. So he sent messengers, saying to them, ''Go and consult Baal-Zebub, the god of Ekron, to see if I will recover from this injury.''

'TYING UP THE STRONG MAN'

Isaiah 49: 24–26

Can plunder be taken from warriors, or captives rescued from the fierce? But this is what the Lord says:

''Yes, captives will be taken from warriors, and plunder retrieved from the fierce; I will contend with those who contend with you, and your children I will save. I will make your oppressors eat their own flesh; they will be drunk on their own blood as with wine. Then all mankind will know that I, the Lord, am your Saviour, your Redeemer, the Mighty One of Jacob.''

Then Jesus entered a house, and again a crowd gathered, so that he and his disciples were not even able to eat. When his family heard about this, they went to take charge of him, for they said, "He is out of his mind." And the teachers of the law who came down from Jerusalem said, "He is possessed by Beelzebub! By the prince of demons he is driving out demons."

So Jesus called them and spoke to them in parables: "How can Satan drive out Satan? If a kingdom is divided against itself, that kingdom cannot stand. If a house is divided against itself, that house cannot stand. And if Satan opposes himself and is divided, he cannot stand, his end has come. In fact, no-one can enter a strong man's house and carry off his possessions unless he first ties up the strong man. Then he can rob his house. I tell you the truth, all the sins and blasphemies of men will be forgiven them. But whoever blasphemes against the Holy Spirit will never be forgiven; he is guilty of an eternal sin

He said this because they were saying, "He has an evil spirit."

Then Jesus mother and brothers arrived. Standing outside, they sent someone in to call him. A crowd was sitting around him, and they told him, "Your mother and brothers are outside looking for you."

"Who are my mother and my brothers?" he asked.

Then he looked at those seated in a circle around him and said, "Here are my mother and my brothers! Whoever does God's will is my brother and sister and mother."

4

On another occasion Jesus began to teach by the lake. The crowd that gathered around him was so large that he got into a boat and sat in it out on the lake, while all the people were along the shore at the water's edge. He taught them many things by parables, and in his teaching said: "Listen! A farmer went out to sow his seed. As he was scattering the seed, some fell along the path, and the birds came and ate it up. Some fell on rocky places, where it did not have much soil. It sprang up quickly, because the soil was shallow. But when the sun came up, the plants were scorched, and they withered because they had no root. Other seed fell among thorns, which grew up and choked the plants, so that they did not bear grain. Still other seed fell on good soil. It came up, grew and produced a crop, multiplying thirty, sixty, or even a hundred times."

Then Jesus said, "He who has ears to hear, let him hear."

A PROPHET'S COMMISSION

Isaiah 6:9–10

He said, "Go and tell this people: 'Be ever hearing, but never understanding; be ever seeing, but never perceiving.' Make the heart of this people calloused; make their ears dull and close their eyes. Otherwise they might see with their eyes, hear with their ears, understand with their hearts, and turn and be healed."

'SECRET OF THE KINGDOM'

Psalm 25:14

The Lord confides in those who fear him; he makes his covenant known to them.

Deuteronomy 29:29

The secret things belong to the Lord our God, but the things revealed belong to us and to our children for ever, that we may follow all the words of this law.

When he was alone, the Twelve and the others around him asked him about the parables. He told them, "The secret of the kingdom of God has been given to you. But to those on the outside everything is said in parables so that,
'they may be ever seeing but never perceiving, and ever hearing but never understanding; otherwise they might turn and be forgiven!'"
Then Jesus said to them, "Don't you understand this parable? How then will you understand any parable? The farmer sows the word. Some people are like seed along the path, where the word is sown. As soon as they hear it, Satan comes and takes away the word that was sown in them. Others, like seed sown on rocky places, hear the word and at once receive it with joy. But since they have no root, they last only a short time. When trouble or persecution comes because of the word, they quickly fall away. Still others, like seed sown among thorns, hear the word; but the worries of this life, the deceitfulness of wealth and the desires for other things come in and choke the word, making it unfruitful. Others, like seed sown on good soil, hear the word, accept it, and produce a crop—thirty, sixty or even a hundred times what was sown."

PARABLES NOT COMPREHENDED

Ezekiel 20:49

Then I said, "Ah, Sovereign Lord! They are saying of me, 'Isn't he just telling parables?'"

UNFRUITFUL SEED

2 Esdras 8:41

"For just as the farmer sows many seeds upon the ground and plants a multitude of seedlings, and yet not all that have been sown will come up in due season, and not all that were planted will take root; so also those who have been sown in the world will not all be saved."

He said to them, "Do you bring in a lamp to put it under a bowl or a bed? Instead, don't you put it on its stand? For whatever is hidden is meant to be disclosed, and whatever is concealed is meant to be brought out into the open. If anyone has ears to hear, let him hear."

"Consider carefully what you hear," he continued. "With the measure you use, it will be measured to you—and even more. Whoever has will be given more; whoever does not have, even what he has will be taken from him."

He also said, "This is what the kingdom of God is like. A man scatters seed on the ground. Night and day, whether he sleeps or gets up, the seed sprouts and grows, though he does not know how. All by itself the soil produces corn—first the stalk, then the ear, then the full kernel in the ear. As soon as the grain is ripe, he puts the sickle to it, because the harvest has come."

CERTAINTY OF HARVEST
Psalm 126:5–6

Those who sow in tears will reap with songs of joy. He who goes out weeping, carrying seed to sow, will return with songs of joy, carrying sheaves with him.

A GREAT TREE

Daniel 4:10–12

These are the visions I saw while lying in my bed: I looked, and there before me stood a tree in the middle of the land. Its height was enormous. The tree grew large and strong and its top touched the sky; it was visible to the ends of the earth. Its leaves were beautiful, its fruit abundant, and on it was food for all. Under it the beasts of the field found shelter, and the birds of the air lived in its branches; from it every creature was fed.

Again he said, "What shall we say the kingdom of God is like, or what parable shall we use to describe it? It is like a mustard seed, which is the smallest seed you plant in the ground. Yet when planted, it grows and becomes the largest of all garden plants, with such big branches that the birds of the air can perch in its shade."

With many similar parables Jesus spoke the word to them, as much as they could understand. He did not say anything to them without using a parable. But when he was alone with his own disciples, he explained everything.

A CEDAR

Ezekiel 17:22–23

This is what the Sovereign Lord says:
''I myself will take a shoot from the very top of a cedar and plant it; I will break off a tender sprig from its topmost shoots and plant it on a high and lofty mountain. On the mountain heights of Israel I will plant it; it will produce branches and bear fruit and become a splendid cedar. Birds of every kind will nest in it; they will find shelter in the shade of its branches.

TEACHING BY PARABLES

Psalm 78:1–2

O my people, hear my teaching; listen to the words of my mouth. I will open my mouth in parables, I will utter hidden things.

WATERS OF CHAOS

Psalm 69:1, 14–15

Save me, O God, for the waters have come up to my neck . . . Rescue me from the mire, do not let me sink; deliver me from those who hate me, from the deep waters. Do not let the floodwaters engulf me or the depth swallow me up or the pit close its mouth over me.

Psalm 89:8–9

O Lord God Almighty, who is like you? You are mighty, O Lord, and your faithfulness surrounds you. You rule over the surging sea; when its waters mount up, you still them.

Psalm 93:3–4

The seas have lifted up, O Lord, the seas have lifted up their voice; the seas have lifted up their pounding waves. Mightier than the thunder of the great waters, mightier than the breakers of the sea – the Lord on high is mighty.

Psalm 46:1–3

God is our refuge and strength, an ever present help in trouble. Therefore we will not fear, though the earth give way and the mountains fall into the heart of the sea, though its waters roar and foam and the mountains quake with their surging.

That day when evening came, he said to his disciples, "Let us go over to the other side." Leaving the crowd behind, they took him along, just as he was, in the boat. There were also other boats with him. A furious squall came up, and the waves broke over the boat, so that it was nearly swamped. Jesus was in the stern, sleeping on a cushion. The disciples woke him and said to him, "Teacher, don't you care if we drown?"

He got up, rebuked the wind and said to the waves, "Quiet! Be still!" Then the wind died down and it was completely calm.

He said to his disciples, "Why are you so afraid? Do you still have no faith?"

They were terrified and asked each other, "Who is this? Even the wind and the waves obey him!"

'SLEEPING'

Psalm 4:8

I will lie down and sleep in peace, for you alone, O Lord, make me dwell in safety.

'WOKE HIM'

Psalm 44: 23–24

Awake, O Lord! Why do you sleep? Rouse yourself! Do not reject us for ever. Why do you hide your face and forget our misery and oppression?

'REBUKED'

Psalm 104:6–7, 9

You covered the earth with the deep as a garment; the waters stood above the mountains. But at your rebuke the waters fled, at the sound of your thunder they took to flight . . . You set a boundary they cannot cross; never again will they cover the earth.

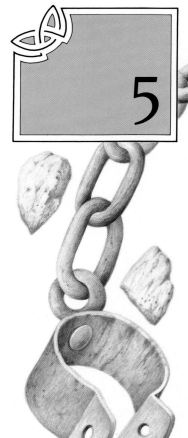

5

They went across the lake to the region of the Gerasenes. When Jesus got out of the boat, a man with an evil spirit came from the tombs to meet him. This man lived in the tombs, and no-one could bind him any more, not even with a chain. For he had often been chained hand and foot, but he tore the chains apart and broke the irons on his feet. No-one was strong enough to subdue him. Night and day among the tombs and in the hills he would cry out and cut himself with stones.

When he saw Jesus from a distance, he ran and fell on his knees in front of him. He shouted at the top of his voice, "What do you want with me, Jesus, Son of the Most High God? Swear to God that you won't torture me!" For Jesus was saying to him, "Come out of this man, you evil spirit!"

Then Jesus asked him, "What is your name?"

"My name is Legion," he replied, "for we are many." And he begged Jesus again and again not to send them out of the area.

A large herd of pigs was feeding on the nearby hillside. The demons begged Jesus, "Send us among the pigs; allow us to go into them." He gave them permission, and the evil spirits came out and went into the pigs. The herd, about two thousand in number, rushed down the steep bank into the lake and were drowned.

PAGAN RITUALS AMONG THE TOMBS

Isaiah 65:2–5

All day long I have held out my hands to an obstinate people, who walk in ways not good, pursuing their own imaginations – a people who continually provoke me to my very face, offering sacrifices in gardens and burning incense on altars of brick; who sit among the graves and spend their nights keeping secret vigil; who eat the flesh of pigs, and whose pots hold broth of unclean meat; who say, "Keep away; don't come near me, for I am too sacred for you!"

DOES GOD WORK BEYOND THE GRAVE?

Psalm 88:10–12

Do you show your wonders to the dead? Do those who are dead rise up and praise you? Is your love declared in the grave, your faithfulness in Destruction? Are your wonders known in the place of darkness, or your righteous deeds in the land of oblivion?

Ezekiel 37:12–14

This is what the Sovereign Lord says:
"O my people, I am going to open your graves and bring you up from them; I will bring you back to the land of Israel. Then you, my people, will know that I am the Lord, when I open your graves and bring you up from them."

'THE DECAPOLIS'
(The Ten Cities)

**Pliny the Elder,
Natural History,
V.xvi.74**

Adjoining Judea on the side of Syria is the region of Decapolis, so called from the number of its towns, though not all writers keep to the same towns in the list; most however include Damascus with its fertile water-meadows that drain the river Chrysorrhoe, Philadelphia, Raphana (all these three withdrawn towards Arabia), Scythopolis . . . where a colony of Scythians are settled, Gadara past which flows the river Yarmuk, Hippo, Dion, Pella rich with its waters, Galasa, Canatha. Between and around these cities run tetrarchies, each of them equal to a kingdom, and they are incorporated into kingdoms . . .

Those tending the pigs ran off and reported this in the town and countryside, and the people went out to see what had happened. When they came to Jesus, they saw the man who had been possessed by the legion of demons, sitting there, dressed and in his right mind; and they were afraid. Those who had seen it told the people what had happened to the demon-possessed man—and told about the pigs as well. Then the people began to plead with Jesus to leave their region.

As Jesus was getting into the boat, the man who had been demon-possessed begged to go with him. Jesus did not let him, but said, "Go home to your family and tell them how much the Lord has done for you, and how he has had mercy on you." So the man went away and began to tell in the Decapolis how much Jesus had done for him. And all the people were amazed.

WITNESS TO NATIONS

Psalm 105:1–2

Give thanks to the Lord, call on his name; make known among the nations what he has done. Sing to him, sing praise to him; tell of all his wonderful acts.

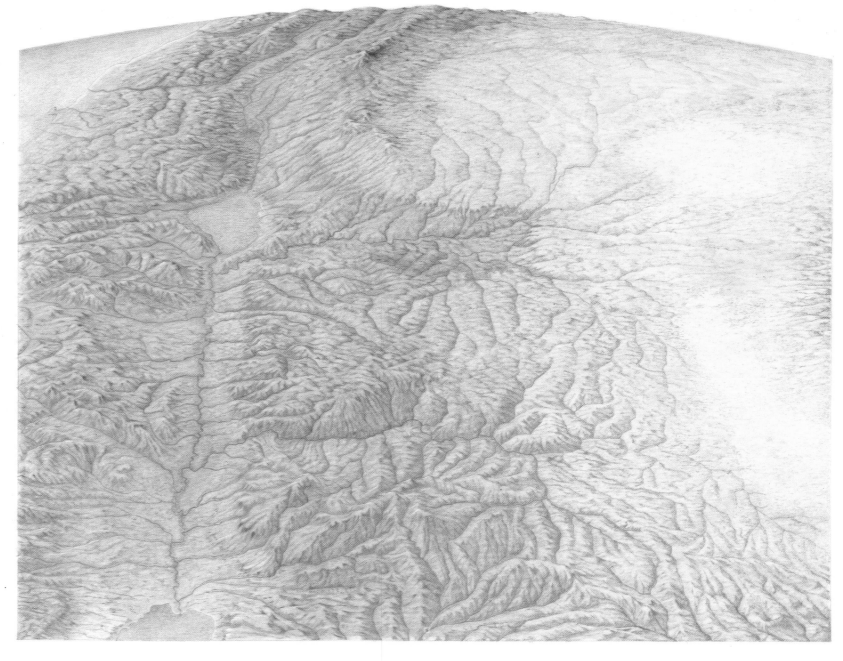

When Jesus had again crossed over by boat to the other side of the lake, a large crowd gathered around him. While he was by the lake, one of the synagogue rulers, named Jairus, came there. Seeing Jesus, he fell at his feet and pleaded earnestly with him, "My little daughter is dying. Please come and put your hands on her so that she will be healed and live." So Jesus went with him.

A large crowd followed and pressed around him. And a woman was there who had been subject to bleeding for twelve years. She had suffered a great deal under the care of many doctors and had spent all she had, yet instead of getting better she grew worse. When she heard about Jesus, she came up behind him in the crowd and touched his cloak, because she thought, "If I just touch his clothes, I will be healed." Immediately her bleeding stopped and she felt in her body that she was freed from her suffering.

At once Jesus realised that power had gone out from him. He turned around in the crowd and asked, "Who touched my clothes?"

"You see the people crowding against you," his disciples answered, "and yet you can ask, 'Who touched me?'"

But Jesus kept looking around to see who had done it. Then the woman, knowing what had happened to her, came and fell at his feet and, trembling with fear, told him the whole truth. He said to her, "Daughter, your faith has healed you. Go in peace and be freed from your suffering."

LAWS ABOUT RITUAL UNCLEANNESS

Leviticus 15:25–30

When a woman has a discharge of blood for many days at a time other than her monthly period or has a discharge that continues beyond her period, she will be unclean as long as she has the discharge, just as in the days of her period. Any bed she lies on while her discharge continues will be unclean, as is her bed during her monthly period, and anything she sits on will be unclean, as during her period. Whoever touches them will be unclean; he must wash his clothes and bathe with water, and he will be unclean till evening. When she is cleansed from her discharge, she must count off seven days, and after that she will be ceremonially clean. On the eighth day she must take two doves or two young pigeons and bring them to the priest at the entrance to the Tent of Meeting. The priest is to sacrifice one for a sin offering and the other for a burnt offering. In this way he will make atonement for her before the Lord for the uncleanness of her discharge.

ELIJAH RESTORES A WIDOW'S SON

1 Kings 17:17–24

The son of the woman who owned the house became ill. He grew worse and worse, and finally stopped breathing. She said to Elijah, ''What do you have against me, man of God? Did you come to remind me of my sin and kill my son?''

''Give me your son,'' Elijah replied. He took him from her arms, carried him to the upper room where he was staying, and laid him on his bed. Then he cried out to the Lord, ''O Lord my God, have you brought tragedy also upon this widow I am staying with, by causing her son to die?'' Then he stretched himself out on the boy three times and cried to the Lord,

''O Lord my God, let this boy's life return to him!'' The Lord heard Elijah's cry, and the boy's life returned to him, and he lived. Elijah picked up the child and carried him down from the room into the house. He gave him to his mother and said, ''Look, your son is alive!''

While Jesus was still speaking, some men came from the house of Jairus, the synagogue ruler. "Your daughter is dead," they said. "Why bother the teacher any more?"

Ignoring what they said, Jesus told the synagogue ruler, "Don't be afraid; just believe."

He did not let anyone follow him except Peter, James and John the brother of James. When they came to the home of the synagogue ruler, Jesus saw a commotion, with people crying and wailing loudly. He went in and said to them, "Why all this commotion and wailing? The child is not dead but asleep." But they laughed at him.

After he put them all out, he took the child's father and mother and the disciples who were with him, and went in where the child was. He took her by the hand and said to her, "Talitha koum!" (which means, "Little girl, I say to you, get up!") Immediately the girl stood up and walked around (she was twelve years old). At this they were completely astonished. He gave strict orders not to let anyone know about this, and told them to give her something to eat.

Then the woman said to Elijah, ''Now I know that you are a man of God and that the word of the Lord from your mouth is the truth.

ELISHA RESTORES A DEAD CHILD

2 Kings 4:32–35

When Elisha reached the house, there was the boy lying dead on his couch. He went in, shut the door on the two of them and prayed to the Lord. Then he got on the bed and lay upon the boy, mouth to mouth, eyes to eyes, hands to hands. As he stretched himself out upon him, the boy's body grew warm. Elisha turned away and walked back and forth in the room and then got onto the bed and stretched out upon him once more. The boy sneezed seven times and opened his eyes.

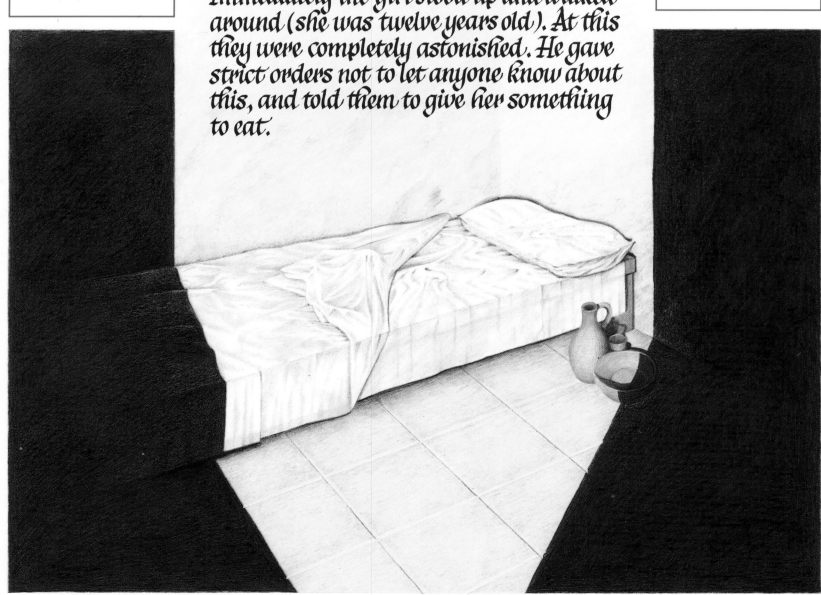

6

THE POOR MAN'S WISDOM

Ecclesiastes 9:13–16

I also saw under the sun this example of wisdom that greatly impressed me: There was once a small city with only a few people in it. And a powerful king came against it, surrounded it, and built huge siegeworks against it. Now there lived in that city a man poor but wise, and he saved the city by his wisdom. But nobody remembered that poor man. So I said, "Wisdom is better than strength." But the poor man's wisdom is despised and his words are no longer heeded.

Jesus left there and went to his home town, accompanied by his disciples. When the Sabbath came, he began to teach in the synagogue, and many who heard him were amazed.

"Where did this man get these things?" they asked. "What's this wisdom that has been given him, that he even does miracles! Isn't this the carpenter? Isn't this Mary's son and the brother of James, Joses, Judas and Simon? Aren't his sisters here with us?" And they took offence at him.

Jesus said to them, "Only in his home town, among his relatives and in his own house is a prophet without honour." He could not do any miracles there, except lay his hands on a few sick people and heal them. And he was amazed at their lack of faith.

MOSES' PROPHECY

Deuteronomy 18:15

The Lord your God will raise up for you a prophet like me from among your own brothers.

Then Jesus went round teaching from village to village. Calling the Twelve to him, he sent them out two by two and gave them authority over evil spirits.

These were his instructions: "Take nothing for the journey except a staff—no bread, no bag, no money in your belts. Wear sandals but not an extra tunic. Whenever you enter a house, stay there until you leave that town. And if any place will not welcome you or listen to you, shake the dust off your feet when you leave, as a testimony against them."

They went out and preached that people should repent. They drove out many demons and anointed many sick people with oil and healed them.

JOHN THE BAPTIST

Josephus 'Antiquities' 18:5.2

John who was called 'Baptist' . . . was a good man and commanded the Jews to exercise virtue, both in righteousness towards one another and in piety towards God, and so to come to baptism . . . Now when many others came in crowds about him (for they were greatly moved by hearing his words) Herod, who feared lest the great influence John had over the people might put it into his power and inclination to raise a rebellion (for they seemed ready to do anything he should advise), thought it best, by putting him to death, to prevent any mischief he might cause . . . Accordingly he was sent a prisoner, out of Herod's suspicious temper, to the fortress called Machaerus . . . and was there put to death.

King Herod heard about this, for Jesus' name had become well known. Some were saying, "John the Baptist has been raised from the dead, and that is why miraculous powers are at work in him."

Others said, "He is Elijah."

And still others claimed, "He is a prophet, like one of the prophets of long ago."

But when Herod heard this, he said, "John, the man I beheaded, has been raised from the dead!"

For Herod himself had given orders to have John arrested, and he had him bound and put in prison. He did this because of Herodias, his brother Philip's wife, whom he had married. For John had been saying to Herod, "It is not lawful for you to have your brother's wife." So Herodias nursed a grudge against John and wanted to kill him. But she was not able to, because Herod feared John and protected him, knowing him to be a righteous and holy man. When Herod heard John, he was greatly puzzled; yet he liked to listen to him.

ELIJAH'S RETURN EXPECTED

Malachi 4:5

See, I will send you the prophet Elijah before that great and terrible day of the Lord comes.

'IT IS NOT LAWFUL'

Leviticus 18:16

Do not have sexual relations with your brother's wife; that would dishonour your brother.

Leviticus 20:21

If a man marries his brother's wife, it is an act of impurity; he has dishonoured his brother. They will be childless.

Finally the opportune time came. On his birthday Herod gave a banquet for his high officials and military commanders and the leading men of Galilee. When the daughter of Herodias came in and danced, she pleased Herod and his dinner guests.

The king said to the girl, "Ask me for anything you want, and I'll give it to you." And he promised her with an oath, "Whatever you ask I will give you, up to half my kingdom."

She went out and said to her mother, "What shall I ask for?"

"The head of John the Baptist," she answered.

At once the girl hurried in to the king with the request: "I want you to give me right now the head of John the Baptist on a platter."

The king was greatly distressed, but because of his oaths and his dinner guests, he did not want to refuse her. So he immediately sent an executioner with orders to bring John's head. The man went, beheaded John in prison, and brought back his head on a platter. He presented it to the girl, and she gave it to her mother. On hearing of this, John's disciples came and took his body and laid it in a tomb.

A KING'S OATH

Esther 5:3

Then the king asked, "What is it, Queen Esther? What is your request? Even up to half the kingdom, it will be given you."

The apostles gathered round Jesus and reported to him all they had done and taught. Then, because so many people were coming and going that they did not even have a chance to eat, he said to them, "Come with me by yourselves to a quiet place and get some rest."

So they went away by themselves in a boat to a solitary place. But many who saw them leaving recognised them and ran on foot from all the towns and got there ahead of them. When Jesus landed and saw a large crowd, he had compassion on them, because they were like sheep without a shepherd. So he began teaching them many things.

'SHEEP WITHOUT A SHEPHERD'

Numbers 27:16–17

May the Lord, the God of the spirits of all mankind, appoint a man over this community to go out and come in before them, one who will lead them out and bring them in, so that the Lord's people will not be like sheep without a shepherd.

EZEKIEL'S PROPHECY AGAINST RULERS

Ezekiel 34:2,4–6

Woe to the shepherds of Israel who only take care of themselves! Should not shepherds take care of the flock? . . . You have not brought back the strays or searched for the lost. You have ruled them harshly and brutally. So they were scattered because there was no shepherd, and when they were scattered they became food for all the wild animals. My sheep wandered over all the mountains and on every high hill.

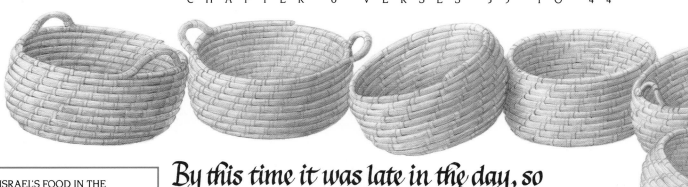

ISRAEL'S FOOD IN THE DESERT

Exodus 16:13–15

That evening quail came and covered the camp, and in the morning there was a layer of dew around the camp. When the dew was gone, thin flakes like frost on the ground appeared on the desert floor. When the Israelites saw it, they said to each other, "What is it?" For they did not know what it was. Moses said to them, "It is the bread the Lord has given you to eat."

Exodus 16:31

The people of Israel called the bread manna. It was white like coriander seed and tasted like wafers made with honey.

By this time it was late in the day, so his disciples came to him. "This is a remote place," they said, "and it's already very late. Send the people away so they can go to the surrounding countryside and villages and buy themselves something to eat."

But he answered, "You give them something to eat."

They said to him, "That would take eight months of a man's wages! Are we to go and spend that much on bread and give it to them to eat?"

"How many loaves do you have?" he asked. "Go and see."

When they found out, they said, "Five—and two fish."

Then Jesus directed them to have all the people sit down in groups on the green grass. So they sat down in groups of hundreds and fifties. Taking the five loaves and the two fish and looking up to heaven, he gave thanks and broke the loaves. Then he gave them to his disciples to set before the people. He also divided the two fish among them all. They all ate and were satisfied, and the disciples picked up twelve basketfuls of broken pieces of bread and fish. The number of the men who had eaten was five thousand.

EZEKIEL'S PROPHECY OF HOPE

Ezekiel 34:11–15

I myself will search for my sheep and look after them . . . I will rescue them from all the places where they were scattered . . . I will bring them into their own land . . . they will feed in a rich pasture on the mountains of Israel. I myself will tend my sheep and make them lie down, declares the Sovereign Lord.

ELISHA'S MIRACULOUS FEEDING

2 Kings 4:42–44

A man came from Baal Shalishah, bringing the man of God twenty loaves of barley bread baked from the first ripe corn, along with some ears of new corn.

"Give it to the people to eat," Elisha said.

"How can I set this before a hundred men?" his servant asked. But Elisha answered, "Give it to the people to eat, for this is what the Lord says: 'They will eat and have some left over.'" Then he set it before them, and they ate and had some left over, according to the word of the Lord.

Immediately Jesus made his disciples get into the boat and go on ahead of him to Bethsaida, while he dismissed the crowd. After leaving them, he went into the hills to pray.

When evening came, the boat was in the middle of the lake, and he was alone on land. He saw the disciples straining at the oars, because the wind was against them. About the fourth watch of the night he went out to them, walking on the lake. He was about to pass by them, but when they saw him walking on the lake, they thought he was a ghost. They cried out, because they all saw him and were terrified.

Immediately he spoke to them and said, "Take courage! It is I. Don't be afraid." Then he climbed into the boat with them, and the wind died down. They were completely amazed, for they had not understood about the loaves; their hearts were hardened.

When they had crossed over, they landed at Gennesaret and anchored there. As soon as they got out of the boat, people recognised Jesus. They ran throughout that whole region and carried the sick on mats to wherever they heard he was. And everywhere he went—into villages, towns or countryside—they placed the sick in the market-places. They begged him to let them touch even the edge of his cloak, and all who touched him were healed.

'WALKING ON THE SEA'

Job 9:8

He alone stretches out the heavens and treads on the waves of the sea.

Psalm 77:19

Your path led through the sea, your way through the mighty waters, though your footprints were not seen.

Isaiah 43:16

This is what the Lord says – he who made a way through the sea, a path through the mighty waters.

ENTERING THE PROMISED LAND

Joshua 3:14–16

When the people broke camp to cross the Jordan, the priests carrying the ark of the covenant went ahead of them. Now the Jordan is in flood all during harvest. Yet as soon as the priests who carried the ark reached the Jordan and their feet touched the water's edge, the water from upstream stopped flowing . . . So the people crossed over opposite Jericho.

7

PHARISEES

Josephus Antiquities 13:10.6

The Pharisees have taught the people a great many observances received from their fathers, which are not written in the law of Moses.

EMPTY RULES

Isaiah 29:13

These people come near to me with their mouth and honour me with their lips, but their hearts are far from me. They worship me in vain; their teachings are but rules taught by men.

HONOUR TO PARENTS

Exodus 20:12

Honour your father and your mother, so that you may live long in the land the Lord your God is giving you.

Exodus 21:17

Anyone who curses his father or mother must be put to death.

The Pharisees and some of the teachers of the law who had come from Jerusalem gathered round Jesus and saw some of his disciples eating food with "unclean"— that is, ceremonially unwashed—hands. (The Pharisees and all the Jews do not eat unless they give their hands a ceremonial washing, holding to the tradition of the elders. When they come from the marketplace they do not eat unless they wash. And they observe many other traditions, such as the washing of cups, pitchers and kettles.)

So the Pharisees and teachers of the law asked Jesus, "Why don't your disciples live according to the tradition of the elders instead of eating their food with 'unclean' hands?"

He replied, "Isaiah was right when he prophesied about you hypocrites; as it is written:
' These people honour me with their lips,
  but their hearts are far from me.
They worship me in vain;
  their teachings are but rules taught by men.'
You have let go of the commands of God and are holding on to the traditions of men."

And he said to them: "You have a fine way of setting aside the commands of God in order to observe your own traditions! For Moses said, 'Honour your father and mother,' and, 'Anyone who curses his father or mother must be put to death.' But you say that if a man says to his father or mother: "Whatever help you might otherwise have received from me is Corban' (that is, a gift devoted to God), then you no longer let him do anything for his father or mother. Thus you nullify the word of God by your tradition that you have handed down. And you do many things like that."

KEEP YOUR VOWS

Deuteronomy 23:21,23

If you make a vow to the Lord your God, do not be slow to pay it, for the Lord your God will certainly demand it of you and you will be guilty of sin . . . Whatever your lips utter you must be sure to do, because you made your vow freely to the Lord your God with your own mouth.

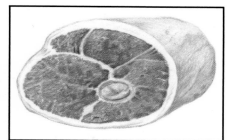

CLEAN AND UNCLEAN FOOD

Deuteronomy 14:3–21

Do not eat any detestable thing. These are the animals you may eat: the ox, the sheep, the goat, the deer, the wild goat, the ibex, the antelope and the mountain sheep. You may eat any animal that has a split hoof divided in two and that chews the cud. However, of those that chew the cud or that have a split hoof completely divided you may not eat the camel, the rabbit or the coney. Although they chew the cud, they do not have a split hoof: they are ceremonially unclean for you. The pig is also unclean; although it has a split hoof, it does not chew the cud. You are not to eat their meat or touch their carcasses. Of all the creatures living in the water, you may eat any that has fins and scales. But anything that does not have fins and scales you may not eat; for you it is unclean. You may eat any clean bird. But these you may not eat: the eagle, the vulture, the black vulture, the red kite, the black kite, any kind of falcon, any kind of raven, the horned owl, the screech owl, the gull, any kind of hawk, the little owl, the great owl, the white owl, the desert owl, the osprey, the cormorant, the stork, any kind of heron, the hoopoe and the bat. All flying insects that swarm are unclean to you; do not eat them. But any winged creature that is clean you may eat. Do not eat anything you find already dead. You may give it to an alien living in any of your towns, and he may eat it, or you may sell it to a foreigner. But you are a people holy to the Lord your God. Do not cook a young goat in its mother's milk.

Again Jesus called the crowd to him and said, "Listen to me, everyone, and understand this. Nothing outside a man can make him 'unclean' by going into him. Rather, it is what comes out of a man that makes him 'unclean'."

After he had left the crowd and entered the house, his disciples asked him about this parable. "Are you so dull?" he asked. "Don't you see that nothing that enters a man from the outside can make him 'unclean'? For it doesn't go into his heart but into his stomach, and then out of his body." (In saying this, Jesus declared all foods "clean".)

He went on: "What comes out of a man is what makes him 'unclean'. For from within, out of men's hearts, come evil thoughts, sexual immorality, theft, murder, adultery, greed, malice, deceit, lewdness, envy, slander, arrogance and folly. All these evils come from inside and make a man 'unclean'."

REGULATIONS TO DO WITH FOOD

Leviticus 11:3–4, 8, 32–35

You may eat any animal that has a split hoof completely divided and that chews the cud. There are some that only chew the cud or only have a split hoof, but you must not eat them . . . You must not eat their meat or touch their carcasses; they are unclean for you. When one of them dies and falls on something, that article, whatever its use, will be unclean, whether it is made of wood, cloth, hide or sackcloth. Put it in water; it will be unclean till evening, and then it will be clean. If one of them falls into a clay pot, everything in it will be unclean, and you must break the pot. Any food that could be eaten but has water on it from such a pot is unclean, and any liquid that could be drunk from it is unclean. Anything that one of their carcasses falls on becomes unclean; an oven or cooking pot must be broken up. They are unclean, and you are to regard them as unclean.

PROPHECIES AGAINST PAGAN TYRE AND SIDON
Ezekiel 28:2,6,8

Son of man, say to the ruler of Tyre: "In the pride of your heart you say, 'I am a god; I sit on the throne of a god in the heart of the seas' . . . Because you think you are wise, as wise as a god, I am going to bring foreigners against you . . . you will die a violent death in the heart of the seas."

SIDON **Ezekiel 28:21**

Son of man, set your face against Sidon; prophesy against her and say: "This is what the Sovereign Lord says: 'I am against you, O Sidon . . . They will know that I am the Lord, when I inflict punishment upon her and show myself holy within her.'"

Ezekiel 28:24

No longer will the people of Israel have malicious neighbours who are painful briers and sharp thorns.

Jesus left that place and went to the vicinity of Tyre. He entered a house and did not want anyone to know it; yet he could not keep his presence secret. In fact, as soon as she heard about him, a woman whose little daughter was possessed by an evil spirit came and fell at his feet. The woman was a Greek, born in Syrian Phoenicia. She begged Jesus to drive the demon out of her daughter.

"First let the children eat all they want," he told her, "for it is not right to take the children's bread and toss it to their dogs."

"Yes, Lord," she replied, "but even the dogs under the table eat the children's crumbs."

Then he told her, "For such a reply, you may go; the demon has left your daughter."

She went home and found her child lying on the bed, and the demon gone.

Then Jesus left the vicinity of Tyre and went through Sidon, down to the Sea of Galilee and into the region of the Decapolis. There some people brought a man to him who was deaf and could hardly talk, and they begged him to place his hand on the man.

After he took him aside, away from the crowd, Jesus put his fingers into the man's ears. Then he spat and touched the man's tongue. He looked up to heaven and with a deep sigh said to him, "Ephphatha!" (which means, "Be opened!"). At this, the man's ears were opened, his tongue was loosened and he began to speak plainly.

Jesus commanded them not to tell anyone. But the more he did so, the more they kept talking about it. People were overwhelmed with amazement. "He has done everything well," they said. "He even makes the deaf hear and the dumb speak."

SIGNS OF GOD'S REDEMPTION

Isaiah 35:4–6

Be strong, do not fear; your God will come, he will come with vengeance; with divine retribution he will come to save you. Then will the eyes of the blind be opened and the ears of the deaf unstopped. Then will the lame leap like a deer, and the mute tongue shout for joy. Water will gush forth in the wilderness and streams in the desert.

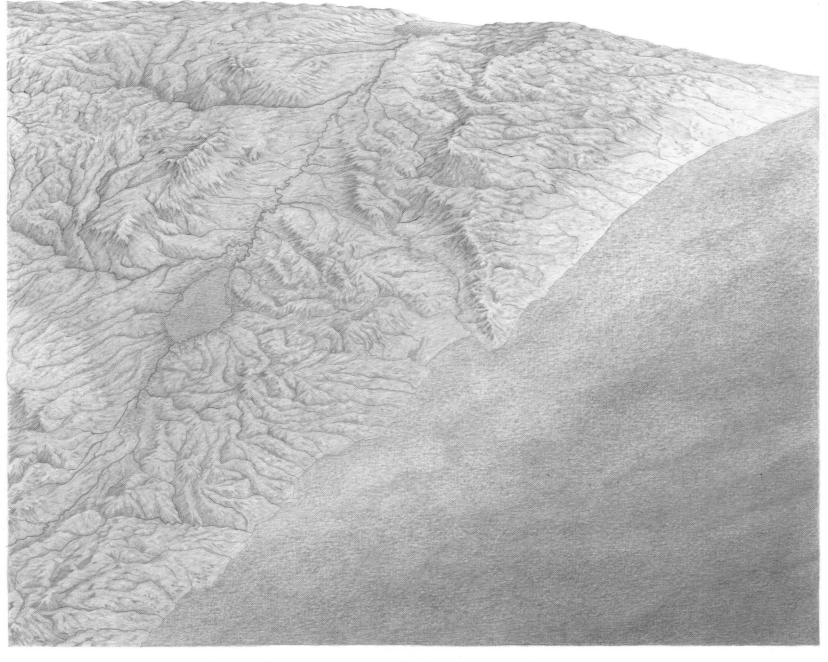

49

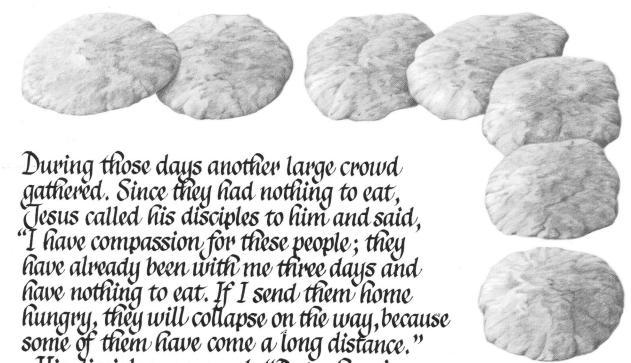

During those days another large crowd gathered. Since they had nothing to eat, Jesus called his disciples to him and said, "I have compassion for these people; they have already been with me three days and have nothing to eat. If I send them home hungry, they will collapse on the way, because some of them have come a long distance."

His disciples answered, "But where in this remote place can anyone get enough bread to feed them?"

"How many loaves do you have?" Jesus asked.

"Seven," they replied.

He told the crowd to sit down on the ground. When he had taken the seven loaves and given thanks, he broke them and gave them to his disciples to set before the people, and they did so. They had a few small fish as well; he gave thanks for them also and told the disciples to distribute them. The people ate and were satisfied. Afterwards the disciples picked up seven basketfuls of broken pieces that were left over. About four thousand men were present. And having sent them away, he got into the boat with his disciples and went to the region of Dalmanutha.

BREAD IN THE DESERT

Psalm 78:19,20,23–25

They spoke against God, saying, "Can God spread a table in the desert? . . . Can he supply meat for his people?" The Lord gave a command to the skies above and opened the doors of the heavens; he rained down manna for the people to eat, he gave them the grain of heaven. Men ate the bread of angels; he sent them all the food they could eat.

Isaiah 38:7–8

"This is the Lord's sign to you that the Lord will do what he has promised: I will make the shadow cast by the sun go back the ten steps it has gone down on the stairway of Ahaz." So the sunlight went back the ten steps it had gone down.

ELIJAH'S SIGN TO KING AHAB

**1 Kings 17:1;
18:36–39,45**

Elijah the Tishbite said to Ahab, "As the Lord, the God of Israel, lives, whom I serve, there will be neither dew nor rain in the next few years except at my word"... At the time of sacrifice, the prophet Elijah stepped forward and prayed: "O Lord, God of Abraham, Isaac and Israel, answer me . . ." Then the fire of the Lord fell and burned up the sacrifice, the wood, the stones, and the soil. When all the people saw this, they fell prostrate and cried, "The Lord he is God!". . . Meanwhile the sky grew black with clouds, the wind rose, and a heavy rain came on.

The Pharisees came and began to question Jesus. To test him, they asked him for a sign from heaven. He sighed deeply and said, "Why does this generation ask for a miraculous sign? I tell you the truth, no sign will be given to it." Then he left them, got back into the boat and crossed to the other side.

'TO TEST HIM'

Psalm 95:7–10

Today, if you hear his voice, do not harden your hearts . . . as you did that day at Massah in the desert, where your fathers tested and tried me, though they had seen what I did. For forty years I was angry with that generation; I said, "They are a people whose hearts go astray, and they have not known my ways."

The disciples had forgotten to bring bread, except for one loaf they had with them in the boat. "Be careful," Jesus warned them. "Watch out for the yeast of the Pharisees and that of Herod."

They discussed this with one another and said, "It is because we have no bread."

Aware of their discussion, Jesus asked them: "Why are you talking about having no bread? Do you still not see or understand? Are your hearts hardened? Do you have eyes but fail to see, and ears but fail to hear? And don't you remember? When I broke the five loaves for the five thousand, how many basketfuls of pieces did you pick up?"

"Twelve," they replied.

"And when I broke the seven loaves for the four thousand, how many basketfuls of pieces did you pick up?"

They answered, "Seven."

He said to them, "Do you still not understand?"

YEAST (symbol of evil)

Leviticus 2:11

"Every grain offering you bring to the Lord must be made without yeast, for you are not to burn any yeast . . . in an offering made to the Lord by fire."

PEOPLE WHO DO NOT HEAR THE PROPHETS

Jeremiah 5:21

Hear this you foolish and senseless people, who have eyes but do not see, who have ears but do not hear.

Ezekiel 12:2,11

Son of man, you are living among a rebellious people. They have eyes to see but do not see and ears to hear but do not hear, for they are a rebellious people . . . Say to them, "I am a sign to you."

They came to Bethsaida, and some people brought a blind man and begged Jesus to touch him. He took the blind man by the hand and led him outside the village. When he had spat on the man's eyes and put his hands on him, Jesus asked, "Do you see anything?"

He looked up and said, "I see people; they look like trees walking around."

Once more Jesus put his hands on the man's eyes. Then his eyes were opened, his sight was restored, and he saw everything clearly. Jesus sent him home, saying, "Don't go into the village."

Jesus and his disciples went on to the villages around Caesarea Philippi. On the way he asked them, "Who do people say I am?"

They replied, "Some say John the Baptist; others say Elijah; and still others, one of the prophets."

"But what about you?" he asked. "Who do you say I am?"

Peter answered, "You are the Christ."

Jesus warned them not to tell anyone about him.

He then began to teach them that the Son of Man must suffer many things and be rejected by the elders, chief priests and teachers of the law, and that he must be killed and after three days rise again. He spoke plainly about this, and Peter took him aside and began to rebuke him.

But when Jesus turned and looked at his disciples, he rebuked Peter. "Out of my sight, Satan!" he said. "You do not have in mind the things of God, but the things of men."

AFTER THREE DAYS

Hosea 6:2

After two days he will revive us; on the third day he will restore us, that we may live in his presence.

Jonah 1:17

But the Lord provided a great fish to swallow Jonah, and Jonah was inside the fish three days and three nights.

ANOINTED ONES
('Christ' means 'anointed one')

Exodus 30:30

Anoint Aaron and his sons and consecrate them so they may serve me as priests.

1 Kings 1:39

Zadok the priest took the horn of oil from the sacred tent and anointed Solomon. Then they sounded the trumpet, and all the people shouted, "Long live King Solomon!"

1 Kings 19:16

Anoint Elisha son of Shaphat from Abel Meholah to succeed you as prophet.

DISCERNING THE PROPHET

Deuteronomy 18:18–22

I will raise up for them a prophet like you from among their brothers; I will put my words in his mouth, and he will tell them everything I command him. If anyone does not listen to my words that the prophet speaks in my name anything I have not commanded him to say, or a prophet who speaks in the name of other gods, must be put to death. You may say to yourselves, "How can we know when a message has not been spoken by the Lord?" If what a prophet proclaims in the name of the Lord does not take place or come true, that is a message the Lord has not spoken. That prophet has spoken presumptuously. Do not be afraid of him.

THE CROSS **Seneca, Epistle 101**

Can any man be found willing to be fastened to the accursed tree, long sickly, already deformed, swelling with ugly weals on shoulder and chest, and drawing the breath of life amid long-drawn-out agony? He would have many excuses for dying before mounting the cross.

Then he called the crowd to him along with his disciples and said: "If anyone would come after me, he must deny himself and take up his cross and follow me. For whoever wants to save his life will lose it, but whoever loses his life for me and for the gospel will save it. What good is it for a man to gain the whole world, yet forfeit his soul? Or what can a man give in exchange for his soul? If anyone is ashamed of me and my words in this adulterous and sinful generation, the Son of Man will be ashamed of him when he comes in his Father's glory with the holy angels."

THE SUFFERING SERVANT

Isaiah 53:1–11

Who has believed our message and to whom has the arm of the Lord been revealed? He grew up before him like a tender shoot, and like a root out of dry ground. He had no beauty or majesty to attract us to him, nothing in his appearance that we should desire him. He was despised and rejected by men, a man of sorrows, and familiar with suffering. Like one from whom men hide their faces he was despised, and we esteemed him not. Surely he took up our infirmities and carried our sorrows, yet we considered him stricken by God, smitten by him and afflicted. But he was pierced for our transgressions, he was crushed for our iniquities; the punishment that brought us peace was upon him, and by his wounds we are healed. We all, like sheep, have gone astray, each of us has turned to his own way;

and the Lord has laid on him the iniquity of us all. He was oppressed and afflicted, yet he did not open his mouth; he was led like a lamb to the slaughter, and as a sheep before her shearers is silent, so he did not open his mouth. By oppression and judgment he was taken away. And who can speak of his descendants? For he was cut off from the land of living; for the transgressions of my people he was stricken. He was assigned a grave with the wicked, and with the rich in his death, though he had done no violence, nor was any deceit in his mouth. Yet it was the Lord's will to crush him and cause him to suffer, and though the Lord makes his life a guilt offering, he will see his offspring and prolong his days, and the will of the Lord will prosper in his hand. After the suffering of his soul, he will see the light of life and be satisfied.

9

And he said to them, "I tell you the truth, some who are standing here will not taste death before they see the kingdom of God come with power."

After six days Jesus took Peter, James and John with him and led them up a high mountain, where they were all alone. There he was transfigured before them. His clothes became dazzling white, whiter than anyone in the world could bleach them. And there appeared before them Elijah and Moses, who were talking with Jesus.

Peter said to Jesus, "Rabbi, it is good for us to be here. Let us put up three shelters—one for you, one for Moses and one for Elijah." (He did not know what to say, they were so frightened.)

Then a cloud appeared and enveloped them, and a voice came from the cloud: "This is my Son, whom I love. Listen to him!"

Suddenly, when they looked round, they no longer saw anyone with them, except Jesus.

GOD'S REVELATION TO MOSES ON MOUNT SINAI

Exodus 24:1–2,15–16

Then God said to Moses, "Come up to the Lord, you and Aaron, Nadab and Abihu . . . Moses alone is to approach the Lord; the others must not come near. And the people may not come up with him . . . When Moses went up on the mountain, the cloud covered it, and the glory of the Lord settled on Mount Sinai. For six days the cloud covered the mountain, and on the seventh day the Lord called to Moses from within the cloud.

'HE WAS TRANSFIGURED'

Exodus 34:29–30

When Moses came down from Mount Sinai . . . he was not aware that his face was radiant because he had spoken with the Lord . . . and they were afraid to come near him.

'MY SON, WHOM I LOVE'

Psalm 2:6–7

I have installed my King on Zion, my holy hill . . . You are my Son.

'LISTEN TO HIM!'

Deuteronomy 18:15

The Lord your God will raise up for you a prophet like me from among your own brothers. You must listen to him.

MOSES AND ELIJAH **Malachi 4:4–5**

Remember the law of my servant Moses, the decrees and laws I gave him at Horeb for all Israel. See, I will send you the prophet Elijah before the great and dreadful day of the Lord comes.

As they were coming down the mountain, Jesus gave them orders not to tell anyone what they had seen until the Son of Man had risen from the dead. They kept the matter to themselves, discussing what "rising from the dead" meant.

And they asked him, "Why do the teachers of the law say that Elijah must come first?"

Jesus replied, "To be sure, Elijah does come first, and restores all things. Why then is it written that the Son of Man must suffer much and be rejected? But I tell you, Elijah has come, and they have done to him everything they wished, just as it is written about him.

When they came to the other disciples, they saw a large crowd around them and the teachers of the law arguing with them. As soon as all the people saw Jesus, they were overwhelmed with wonder and ran to greet him.

"What are you arguing with them about?" he asked.

A man in the crowd answered, "Teacher, I brought you my son, who is possessed by a spirit that has robbed him of speech. Whenever it seizes him, it throws him to the ground. He foams at the mouth, gnashes his teeth and becomes rigid. I asked your disciples to drive out the spirit, but they could not."

"O unbelieving generation," Jesus replied, "How long shall I stay with you? How long shall I put up with you? Bring the boy to me."

So they brought him. When the spirit saw Jesus, it immediately threw the boy into a convulsion. He fell to the ground and rolled around, foaming at the mouth.

Jesus asked the boy's father, "How long has he been like this?"

"From childhood," he answered. "It has often thrown him into fire or water to kill him. But if you can do anything, take pity on us and help us."

" 'If you can'?" said Jesus. "Everything is possible for him who believes."

Immediately the boy's father exclaimed, "I do believe; help me overcome my unbelief!"

When Jesus saw that a crowd was running to the scene, he rebuked the evil spirit. "You deaf and dumb spirit," he said, "I command you, come out of him and never enter him again."

The spirit shrieked, convulsed him violently and came out. The boy looked so much like a corpse that many said, "He's dead." But Jesus took him by the hand and lifted him to his feet, and he stood up.

After Jesus had gone indoors, his disciples asked him privately, "Why couldn't we drive it out?"

He replied, "This kind can come out only by prayer."

UNBELIEVING ISRAEL

Exodus 32:1,19–20

When the people saw that Moses was so long in coming down from the mountain, they gathered round Aaron and said, ''Come, make us gods who will go before us . . .'' When Moses approached the camp and saw the calf and the dancing, his anger burned . . . And he took the calf they had made and burned it in the fire; then he ground it to powder, scattered it on the water and made the Israelites drink it.

THE PURPOSE OF MOSES' LAWS

Psalm 78:5–7

God established the law in Israel, which he commanded our forefathers to teach their children, so that the next generation would know them . . . Then they would put their trust in God . . . They would not be like their forefathers – a stubborn and rebellious generation, whose hearts were not loyal to God, whose spirits were not faithful to him.

They left that place and passed through Galilee. Jesus did not want anyone to know where they were, because he was teaching his disciples. He said to them, "The Son of Man is going to be betrayed into the hands of men. They will kill him, and after three days he will rise." But they did not understand what he meant and were afraid to ask him about it.

They came to Capernaum. When he was in the house, he asked them, "What were you arguing about on the road?" But they kept quiet because on the way they had argued about who was the greatest.

Sitting down, Jesus called the Twelve and said, "If anyone wants to be first, he must be the very last, and the servant of all."

He took a little child and had him stand among them. Taking him in his arms, he said to them, "Whoever welcomes one of these little children in my name welcomes me; and whoever welcomes me does not welcome me but the one who sent me."

"Teacher," said John, "we saw a man driving out demons in your name and we told him to stop, because he was not one of us."

"Do not stop him," Jesus said. "No-one who does a miracle in my name can in the next moment say anything bad about me, for whoever is not against us is for us. I tell you the truth, anyone who gives you a cup of water in my name because you belong to Christ will certainly not lose his reward."

'DON'T STOP THEM'

Numbers 11:27–29

A young man ran up and told Moses, ''Eldad and Medad are prophesying in the camp.'' Joshua son of Nun, who had been Moses' assistant since youth, spoke up and said, ''Moses, my lord, stop them!'' But Moses replied, ''Are you jealous for my sake? I wish that all the Lord's people were prophets and that the Lord would put his Spirit on them.''

"And if anyone causes one of these little ones who believe in me to sin, it would be better for him to be thrown into the sea with a large millstone tied around his neck. If your hand causes you to sin, cut it off. It is better for you to enter life maimed than with two hands to go into hell, where the fire never goes out. And if your foot causes you to sin, cut it off. It is better for you to enter life crippled than to have two feet and be thrown into hell. And if your eye causes you to sin, pluck it out. It is better for you to enter the kingdom of God with one eye than to have two eyes and be thrown into hell, where
  'their worm does not die,
    and the fire is not quenched.'
Everyone will be salted with fire.
  "Salt is good, but if it loses its saltiness, how can you make it salty again? Have salt in yourselves, and be at peace with each other."

WORM AND FIRE
Isaiah 66:24

They will go out and look upon the dead bodies of those who rebelled against me; their worm will not die, nor will their fire be quenched, and they will be loathsome to all mankind.

10

Jesus then left that place and went into the region of Judea and across the Jordan. Again crowds of people came to him, and as was his custom, he taught them.

Some Pharisees came and tested him by asking, "Is it lawful for a man to divorce his wife?"

"What did Moses command you?" he replied.

They said, "Moses permitted a man to write a certificate of divorce and send her away."

"It was because your hearts were hard that Moses wrote you this law," Jesus replied. "But at the beginning of creation God 'made them male and female'. 'For this reason a man will leave his father and mother and be united to his wife, and the two will become one flesh.' So they are no longer two, but one. Therefore what God has joined together, let man not separate."

When they were in the house again, the disciples asked Jesus about this. He answered, "Anyone who divorces his wife and marries another woman commits adultery against her. And if she divorces her husband and marries another man, she commits adultery."

People were bringing little children to Jesus to have him touch them, but the disciples rebuked them. When Jesus saw this, he was indignant. He said to them, "Let the little children come to me, and do not hinder them, for the kingdom of God belongs to such as these. I tell you the truth, anyone who will not receive the kingdom of God like a little child will never enter it." And he took the children in his arms, put his hands on them and blessed them.

MOSES' DIVORCE LAWS

Deuteronomy 24:1–4

If a man marries a woman who becomes displeasing to him because he finds something indecent about her, and he writes her a certificate of divorce, gives it to her and sends her from his house, and if after she leaves his house she becomes the wife of another man, and her second husband dislikes her, and writes her a certificate of divorce, gives it to her and sends her from his house, or if he dies, then her first husband, who divorced her, is not allowed to marry her again after she has been defiled. That would be detestable in the eyes of the Lord.

GOD'S PURPOSE FOR MARRIAGE

Genesis 1:27

So God created man in his own image, in the image of God he created him; male and female he created them.

Genesis 2:24

For this reason a man will leave his father and mother and be united to his wife, and they will become one flesh.

As Jesus started on his way, a man ran up to him and fell on his knees before him. "Good teacher," he asked, "what must I do to inherit eternal life?"

"Why do you call me good?" Jesus answered. "No-one is good—except God alone. You know the commandments: 'Do not murder, do not commit adultery, do not steal, do not give false testimony, do not defraud, honour your father and mother.'"

"Teacher," he declared, "all these I have kept since I was a boy."

Jesus looked at him and loved him. "One thing you lack," he said. "Go, sell everything you have and give to the poor, and you will have treasure in heaven. Then come, follow me."

At this the man's face fell. He went away sad, because he had great wealth.

Jesus looked around and said to his disciples, "How hard it is for the rich to enter the kingdom of God!"

'THE COMMANDMENTS'

Exodus 20:12–16

Honour your father and your mother, so that you may live long in the land the Lord your God is giving you.

You shall not murder.

You shall not commit adultery.

You shall not steal.

You shall not give false testimony against your neighbour.

Leviticus 19:13

Do not defraud your neighbour or rob him.

'SINCE I WAS A BOY'

Deuteronomy 6:6–7

These commandments that I give you today are to be upon your hearts. Impress them on your children. Talk about them when you sit at home and when you walk along the road, when you lie down and when you get up.

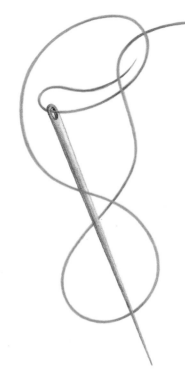

The disciples were amazed at his words. But Jesus said again, "Children, how hard it is to enter the kingdom of God! It is easier for a camel to go through the eye of a needle than for a rich man to enter the kingdom of God."

The disciples were even more amazed, and said to each other, "Who then can be saved?"

Jesus looked at them and said, "With man this is impossible, but not with God; all things are possible with God."

Peter said to him, "We have left everything to follow you!"

"I tell you the truth," Jesus replied, "no-one who has left home or brothers or sisters or mother or father or children or fields for me and the gospel will fail to receive a hundred times as much in this present age (homes, brothers, sisters, mothers, children and fields—and with them, persecutions) and in the age to come, eternal life. But many who are first will be last, and the last first."

'POSSIBLE WITH GOD'

Genesis 18:14

Is anything too hard for the Lord? I will return to you at the appointed time next year and Sarah will have a son.

Job 42:2

I know that you can do all things; no plan of yours can be thwarted.

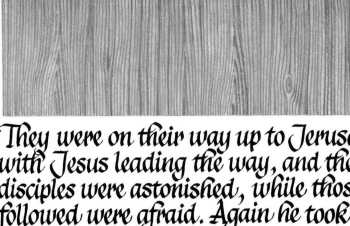

They were on their way up to Jerusalem, with Jesus leading the way, and the disciples were astonished, while those who followed were afraid. Again he took the Twelve aside and told them what was going to happen to him. "We are going up to Jerusalem," he said, "and the Son of Man will be betrayed to the chief priests and teachers of the law. They will condemn him to death and will turn him over to the Gentiles, who will mock him and spit on him, flog him and kill him. Three days later he will rise."

Then James and John, the sons of Zebedee, came to him. "Teacher," they said, "we want you to do for us whatever we ask."

"What do you want me to do for you?" he asked.

They replied, "Let one of us sit at your right and the other at your left in your glory."

"You don't know what you are asking," Jesus said. "Can you drink the cup I drink or be baptised with the baptism I am baptised with?"

"We can," they answered.

Jesus said to them, "You will drink the cup I drink and be baptised with the baptism I am baptised with, but to sit at my right or left is not for me to grant. These places belong to those for whom they have been prepared."

When the ten heard about this, they became indignant with James and John. Jesus called them together and said, "You know that those who are regarded as rulers of the Gentiles lord it over them, and their high officials exercise authority over them. Not so with you. Instead, whoever wants to become great among you must be your servant, and whoever wants to be first must be slave of all. For even the Son of Man did not come to be served, but to serve, and to give his life as a ransom for many."

'DRINK THE CUP'

Psalm 75:8

In the hand of the Lord is a cup full of foaming wine mixed with spices; he pours it out, and all the wicked of the earth drink it down to its very dregs.

Pseudo-Manetha, Apotelesmatica 4:198ff

Punished with limbs outstretched, they see the stake as their fate: they are fastened and nailed to it in the most bitter torment, evil food for birds of prey and grim pickings for dogs.

'BE BAPTISED'

Psalm 69:1–2

Save me, O God, for the waters have come up to my neck. I sink in the miry depths, where there is no foothold. I have come from the deep waters, the floods engulf me.

'RANSOM'

4 Maccabees 6:29

Make my blood their purification, and take my life in exchange for theirs.

'FOR MANY'

Isaiah 53:11–12

By his knowledge my righteous servant will justify many, and he will bear their iniquities . . . because he poured out his life unto death, and was numbered with the transgressors. For he bore the sin of many, and made intercession for the transgressors.

Then they came to Jericho. As Jesus and his disciples, together with a large crowd, were leaving the city, a blind man, Bartimaeus (that is, the Son of Timaeus), was sitting by the roadside begging. When he heard that it was Jesus of Nazareth, he began to shout, "Jesus, Son of David, have mercy on me!"

Many rebuked him and told him to be quiet, but he shouted all the more, "Son of David, have mercy on me!"

Jesus stopped and said, "Call him."

So they called to the blind man, "Cheer up! On your feet! He's calling you." Throwing his cloak aside, he jumped to his feet and came to Jesus.

"What do you want me to do for you?" Jesus asked him.

The blind man said, "Rabbi, I want to see."

"Go," said Jesus, "your faith has healed you." Immediately he received his sight and followed Jesus along the road.

11

A PROPHECY AWAITING
FULFILMENT

Zechariah 9:9–10

Rejoice greatly, O
Daughter of Zion! Shout,
daughter of Jerusalem!
See, your king comes to
you, righteous and having
salvation; gentle and
riding on a donkey, on a
colt, the foal of a donkey. I
will take away the chariots
from Ephraim and the
war-horses from
Jerusalem, and the battle-
bow will be broken. He
will proclaim peace to the
nations. His rule will
extend from sea to sea
and from the River to the
ends of the earth.

'THE COMING KINGDOM OF
OUR FATHER DAVID'

Jeremiah 30:8–9

''In that day,'' declares the
Lord Almighty, ''I will
break the yoke off their
necks and will tear off
their bonds; no longer will
foreigners enslave them.
Instead, they will serve the
Lord their God and David
their king, whom I will
raise up for them.''

As they approached Jerusalem and came to Bethphage and Bethany at the Mount of Olives, Jesus sent two of his disciples, saying to them, "Go to the village ahead of you, and, just as you enter it, you will find a colt tied there, which no-one has ever ridden. Untie it and bring it here. If anyone asks you, 'Why are you doing this?' tell him, 'The Lord needs it and will send it back here shortly.' "

They went and found a colt outside in the street, tied at a doorway. As they untied it, some people standing there asked, "What are you doing, untying that colt?" They answered as Jesus had told them to, and the people let them go. When they brought the colt to Jesus and threw their cloaks over it, he sat on it. Many people spread their cloaks on the road, while others spread branches they had cut in the fields. Those who went ahead and those who followed shouted,

"Hosanna! Blessed is he who comes in the name of the Lord! Blessed is the coming kingdom of our father David! Hosanna in the highest!"

Jesus entered Jerusalem and went to the temple. He looked around at everything, but since it was already late, he went out to Bethany with the Twelve.

'SPREAD THEIR CLOAKS'

2 Kings 9:13

They hurried and took
their cloaks and spread
them under him on the
bare steps. Then they blew
the trumpet and shouted,
''Jehu is king!''

'HOSANNA!'

Psalm 118:25–26

O Lord, save us; O Lord,
grant us success. Blessed
is he who comes in the
name of the Lord. From
the house of the Lord we
bless you.

Psalm 20:9

O Lord, save the king!
Answer us when we call.

ANCIENT FORM OF ADDRESS
TO A KING

2 Samuel 14:4

When the woman from
Tekoa went to the king,
she fell with her face to
the ground to pay him
honour, and she said,
''Help me, O king!''

2 Kings 6:26

As the king of Israel was
passing by on the wall, a
woman cried to him,
''Help me, my lord the
king!''

ISRAEL, A FIG TREE

Jeremiah 8:13

"I will take away their harvest," declares the Lord. "There will be no grapes on the vine. There will be no figs on the tree, and their leaves will wither. What I have given them will be taken from them."

The next day as they were leaving Bethany, Jesus was hungry. Seeing in the distance a fig-tree in leaf, he went to find out if it had any fruit. When he reached it, he found nothing but leaves, because it was not the season for figs. Then he said to the tree, "May no-one ever eat fruit from you again." And his disciples heard him say it.

ALLEGORY OF TREES

Hosea 9:10

When I found Israel, it was like finding grapes in the desert; when I saw your fathers, it was like seeing the early fruit on the fig-tree. But when they came to Baal Peor, they consecrated themselves to that shameful idol and became as vile as the thing they loved.

Ezekiel 17:24

All the trees of the field will know that I the Lord bring down the tall tree and make the low tree grow tall. I dry up the green tree and make the dry tree flourish. I the Lord have spoken, and I will do it.

On reaching Jerusalem, Jesus entered the temple area and began driving out those who were buying and selling there. He overturned the tables of the money changers and the benches of those selling doves, and would not allow anyone to carry merchandise through the temple courts. And as he taught them, he said, "Is it not written:

'My house will be called a house of prayer for all nations'?

But you have made it 'a den of robbers.'"

The chief priests and the teachers of the law heard this and began looking for a way to kill him, for they feared him, because the whole crowd was amazed at his teaching.

When evening came, they went out of the city.

PROPHECIES OF TEMPLE REFORM

Malachi 3:1–3

"See, I will send my messenger, who will prepare the way before me. Then suddenly the Lord you are seeking will come to his temple; the messenger of the covenant, whom you desire, will come," says the Lord Almighty . . . But who can stand when he appears . . . For he will purify the Levites and refine them like gold and silver. Then the Lord will have men who will bring offerings in righteousness.

Zechariah 14:21

On that day there will no longer be a merchant in the house of the Lord Almighty.

Hosea 9:15

Because of their sinful deeds, I will drive them out of my house. I will no longer love them; all their leaders are rebellious.

Jeremiah 7:2–4,11

Stand at the gate of the Lord's house and there proclaim this message: "Hear the word of the Lord, all you people of Judah who come through these gates to worship the Lord. Reform your ways . . . Do not trust in deceptive words and say, 'This is the temple of the Lord, the temple of the Lord!' . . . Has this house, which bears my Name, become a den of robbers to you? But I have been watching!" declares the Lord.

THE TEMPLE OPEN TO FOREIGNERS

Isaiah 56:6–7

And foreigners who bind themselves to the Lord to serve him, to love the name of the Lord, and to worship him, all who keep the Sabbath without desecrating it and who hold fast to my covenant – these I will bring to my holy mountain and give them joy in my house of prayer. Their burnt offerings and sacrifices will be accepted on my altar; for my house will be called a house of prayer for all nations.

In the morning, as they went along, they saw the fig-tree withered from the roots. Peter remembered and said to Jesus, "Rabbi, look! The fig-tree you cursed has withered!"

"Have faith in God," Jesus answered. "I tell you the truth, if anyone says to this mountain, 'Go, throw yourself into the sea,' and does not doubt in his heart but believes that what he says will happen, it will be done for him. Therefore I tell you, whatever you ask for in prayer, believe that you have received it, and it will be yours. And when you stand praying, if you hold anything against anyone, forgive him, so that your Father in heaven may forgive you your sins."

They arrived again in Jerusalem, and while Jesus was walking in the temple courts, the chief priests, the teachers of the law and the elders came to him. "By what authority are you doing these things?" they asked. "And who gave you authority to do this?"

Jesus replied, "I will ask you one question. Answer me, and I will tell you by what authority I am doing these things. John's baptism—was it from heaven, or from men? Tell me!"

They discussed it among themselves and said, "If we say, 'From heaven,' he will ask, 'Then why didn't you believe him?' But if we say, 'From men'…" (They feared the people, for everyone held that John really was a prophet.)

So they answered Jesus, "We don't know."

Jesus said, "Neither will I tell you by what authority I am doing these things."

JEREMIAH QUESTIONED

Jeremiah 26:8–9

As soon as Jeremiah finished telling all the people everything the Lord had commanded him to say, the priests, the prophets and all the people seized him and said, "You must die! Why do you prophesy in the Lord's name that this house will be like Shiloh and this city will be desolate and deserted?"

12

He then began to speak to them in parables: "A man planted a vineyard. He put a wall around it, dug a pit for the winepress and built a watchtower. Then he rented the vineyard to some farmers and went away on a journey. At harvest time he sent a servant to the tenants to collect from them some of the fruit of the vineyard. But they seized him, beat him and sent him away empty-handed. Then he sent another servant to them; they struck this man on the head and treated him shamefully. He sent still another, and that one they killed. He sent many others; some of them they beat, others they killed.

He had one left to send, a son, whom he loved. He sent him last of all saying, "They will respect my son.'

But the tenants said to one another, 'This is the heir. Come, let's kill him, and the inheritance will be ours.' So they took him and killed him, and threw him out of the vineyard. What then will the owner of the vineyard do? He will come and kill those tenants and give the vineyard to others. Haven't you read this scripture:

"The stone the builders rejected
has become the capstone;
the Lord has done this, and it is
marvellous in our eyes'?"

Then they looked for a way to arrest him because they knew he had spoken the parable against them. But they were afraid of the crowd; so they left him and went away.

Later they sent some of the Pharisees and Herodians to Jesus to catch him in his words. They came to him and said, "Teacher, we know you are a man of integrity. You aren't swayed by men, because you pay no attention to who they are; but you teach the way of God in accordance with the truth. Is it right to pay taxes to Caesar or not? Should we pay or shouldn't we?"

But Jesus knew their hypocrisy. "Why are you trying to trap me?" he asked. "Bring me a denarius and let me look at it." They brought the coin, and he asked them, "Whose portrait is this? And whose inscription?"

"Caesar's," they replied.

Then Jesus said to them, "Give to Caesar what is Caesar's and to God what is God's."

And they were amazed at him.

'MOSES WROTE . . .'

Deuteronomy 25:5–6

If brothers are living together and one of them dies without a son, his widow must not marry outside the family. Her husband's brother shall take her and marry her and fulfil the duty of a brother-in-law to her. The first son she bears shall carry on the name of the dead brother so that his name will not be blotted out from Israel.

SADDUCEES

Josephus, Antiquities 13:10.6 and 17:1.4

The Sadducees say that we are to consider obligatory those observances which are in the written word, but are not to observe what are derived from the traditions of the fathers.

The doctrine of the Sadducees is this: that souls die with the bodies; and they do not observe anything besides what the law enjoins; they consider it virtuous to dispute with teachers of philosophy.

THE BURNING BUSH

Exodus 3:1–6

Now Moses was tending the flock of Jethro his father-in-law, the priest of Midian, and he led the flock to the far side of the desert and came to Horeb, the mountain of God. There the angel of the Lord appeared to him in flames of fire from within a bush. Moses saw that though the bush was on fire it did not burn up. So Moses thought, "I will go over and see this strange sight – why the bush does not burn up." When the Lord saw that he had gone over to look, God called to him from within the bush, "Moses! Moses!" And Moses said, "Here I am."
"Do not come any closer," God said.
"Take off your sandals, for the place where you are standing is holy ground." Then he said, "I am the God of your fathers, the God of Abraham, the God of Isaac and the God of Jacob." At this, Moses hid his face, because he was afraid to look at God.

Then the Sadducees, who say there is no resurrection, came to him with a question. "Teacher," they said, "Moses wrote for us that if a man's brother dies and leaves a wife but no children, the man must marry the widow and have children for his brother. Now there were seven brothers. The first one married and died without leaving any children. The second one married the widow, but he also died, leaving no child. It was the same with the third. In fact, none of the seven left any children. Last of all, the woman died too. At the resurrection whose wife will she be, since the seven were married to her?"

Jesus replied, "Are you not in error because you do not know the Scriptures or the power of God? When the dead rise, they will neither marry nor be given in marriage; they will be like the angels in heaven. Now about the dead rising—have you not read in the book of Moses, in the account of the bush, how God said to him, 'I am the God of Abraham, the God of Isaac, and the God of Jacob'? He is not the God of the dead, but of the living. You are badly mistaken!"

THE EARLIEST CLEAR REFERENCE TO RESURRECTION

Daniel 12:2

Multitudes who sleep in the dust of the earth will awake: some to everlasting life, others to shame and everlasting contempt.

THE SHEMA

Deuteronomy 6:4–5

Hear, O Israel: The Lord our God, the Lord is one. Love the Lord your God with all your heart and with all your soul and with all your strength.

LOVE FOR NEIGHBOUR **Leviticus** 19:18

Do not seek revenge or bear a grudge against one of your people, but love your neighbour as yourself. I am the Lord.

One of the teachers of the law came and heard them debating. Noticing that Jesus had given them a good answer, he asked him, "Of all the commandments, which is the most important?"

"The most important one," answered Jesus, "is this: 'Hear, O Israel, the Lord our God, the Lord is one. Love the Lord your God with all your heart and with all your soul and with all your mind and with all your strength.' The second is this: 'Love your neighbour as yourself.' There is no commandment greater than these."

"Well said, teacher," the man replied. "You are right in saying that God is one and there is no other but him. To love him with all your heart, with all your understanding and with all your strength, and to love your neighbour as yourself is more important than all burnt offerings and sacrifices."

When Jesus saw that he had answered wisely, he said to him, "You are not far from the kingdom of God." And from then on no-one dared ask him any more questions.

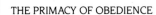

THE PRIMACY OF OBEDIENCE

Hosea 6:6

I desire mercy, not sacrifice, and acknowledgment of God rather than burnt offerings.

1 Samuel 15:22

Does the Lord delight in burnt offerings and sacrifices as much as in obeying the voice of the Lord? To obey is better than sacrifice, and to heed is better than the fat of rams.

While Jesus was teaching in the temple courts, he asked, "How is it that the teachers of the law say that the Christ is the son of David? David himself, speaking by the Holy Spirit, declared:

"The Lord said to my Lord: "Sit at my right hand until I put your enemies under your feet.""

David himself calls him 'Lord.' How then can he be his son?"

The large crowd listened to him with delight. As he taught, Jesus said, "Watch out for the teachers of the law. They like to walk around in flowing robes and be greeted in the market-places, and have the most important seats in the synagogues and the places of honour at banquets. They devour widows' houses and for a show make lengthy prayers. Such men will be punished most severely."

Jesus sat down opposite the place where the offerings were put and watched the crowd putting their money into the temple treasury. Many rich people threw in large amounts. But a poor widow came and put in two very small copper coins, worth only a fraction of a penny.

Calling his disciples to him, Jesus said, "I tell you the truth, this poor widow has put more into the treasury than all the others. They all gave out of their wealth; but she, out of her poverty, put in everything—all she had to live on."

13

As he was leaving the temple, one of his disciples said to him, "Look, Teacher! What massive stones! What magnificent buildings!"

"Do you see all these great buildings?" replied Jesus. "Not one stone here will be left on another; every one will be thrown down."

As Jesus was sitting on the Mount of Olives opposite the temple, Peter, James, John and Andrew asked him privately, "Tell us, when will these things happen? And what will be the sign that they are all about to be fulfilled?"

EARLIER PROPHECIES OF THE TEMPLE'S DESTRUCTION

Jeremiah 26:6,18

I will make this house like Shiloh and this city an object of cursing among all the nations of the earth. . . . Micah of Moresheth prophesied in the days of Hezekiah, king of Judah. He told all the people of Judah, "This is what the Lord Almighty says: 'Zion will be ploughed like a field, Jerusalem will become a heap of rubble, the temple hill a mound overgrown with thickets.'"

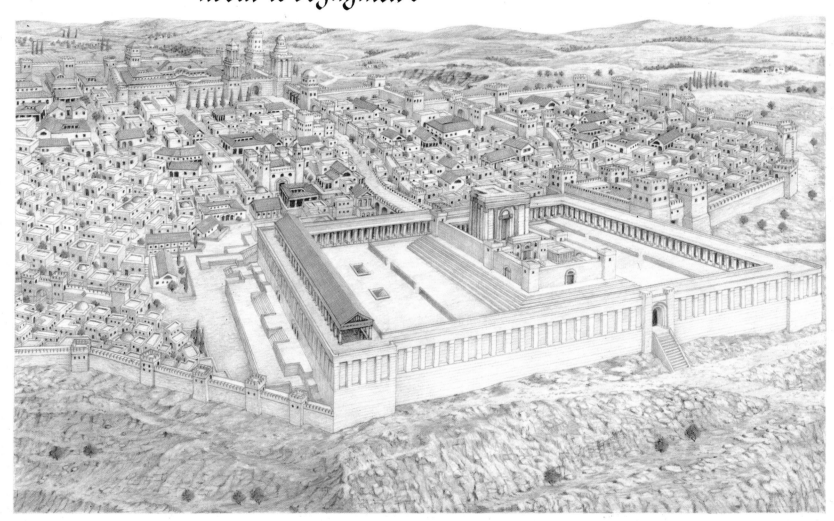

THE TEMPLE'S DESTRUCTION IN AD70

Josephus Jewish War, vi, 230ff

For six days the most powerful battering-ram of all had been pounding the wall incessantly without result; this like the others made no impression on stones so huge and so perfectly bonded. At the northern gate a second team attempted to undermine the foundations, and by tremendous efforts they did lever out the stones in

front; but the inner stones supported the weight and the gate stood firm, till despairing of all attempts with engines and crowbars they set up ladders against the colonnades . . . By now the soldiers were setting fire to the gates. The silver melted and ran, quickly exposing the woodwork to the flames, which were carried from there in a solid wall and fastened onto the colonnades. When the Jews saw the ring of fire, they lost all power of body and mind . . .

Jesus said to them: "Watch out that no-one deceives you. Many will come in my name, claiming, 'I am he,' and will deceive many. When you hear of wars and rumours of wars, do not be alarmed. Such things must happen, but the end is still to come. Nation will rise against nation, and kingdom against kingdom. There will be earthquakes in various places, and famines. These are the beginning of birth pains.

"You must be on your guard. You will be handed over to the local councils and flogged in the synagogues. On account of me you will stand before governors and kings as witnesses to them. And the gospel must first be preached to all nations. Whenever you are arrested and brought to trial, do not worry beforehand about what to say. Just say whatever is given you at the time, for it is not you speaking, but the Holy Spirit.

"Brother will betray brother to death, and a father his child. Children will rebel against their parents and have them put to death. All men will hate you because of me, but he who stands firm to the end will be saved.

'BIRTH-PAINS'

Isaiah 26:17

As a woman with child and about to give birth writhes and cries out in her pain, so were we in your presence, O Lord.

Jeremiah 22:23

You who live in 'Lebanon' (a palace in Jerusalem), who are nestled in cedar buildings, how you will groan when pangs come upon you, pain like that of a woman in labour!

Micah 4:9–10

Why do you now cry aloud – have you no king? Has your counsellor perished, that pain seizes you like that of a woman in labour? Writhe in agony, O Daughter of Zion, like a woman in labour, for now you must leave the city to camp in the open field. You will go to Babylon.

1 Thessalonians 5:3

While people are saying, "Peace and safety," destruction will come on them suddenly, as labour pains on a pregnant woman, and they will not escape.

VISIONS OF THE FUTURE

2 Esdras 9:1–4

Measure carefully in your mind, and when you see that a certain part of the predicted signs are past, then you will know that it is the very time when the Most High is about to visit the world which he has made. So when there shall appear in the world earthquakes, tumult of peoples, intrigues of nations, wavering of leaders, confusion of princes, then you will know that it was of these that the Most High spoke . . . from the beginning.

2 Esdras 13:31–32

And they shall plan to make war against one another, city against city, place against place, people against people, and kingdom against kingdom. When these things come to pass . . . then my Son will be revealed.

"When you see 'the abomination that causes desolation' standing where it does not belong—let the reader understand—then let those who are in Judea flee to the mountains. Let no-one on the roof of his house go down or enter the house to take anything out. Let no-one in the field go back to get his cloak. How dreadful it will be in those days for pregnant women and nursing mothers! Pray that this will not take place in winter, because those will be days of distress unequalled from the beginning, when God created the world, until now—and never to be equalled again. If the Lord had not cut short those days, no-one would survive. But for the sake of the elect, whom he has chosen, he has shortened them. At that time, if anyone says to you, 'Look, here is the Christ!' or, 'Look, there he is!' do not believe it. For false Christs and false prophets will appear and perform signs and miracles to deceive the elect—if that were possible. So be on your guard; I have told you everything ahead of time.'

'DISTRESS UNEQUALLED FROM THE BEGINNING'

Daniel 12:1

At that time Michael, the great prince who protects your people, will arise. There will be a time of distress such as has not happened from the beginning of nations until then. But at that time your people – everyone whose name is found written in the book – will be delivered.

'ABOMINATION THAT CAUSES DESOLATION'

Daniel 11:31

His armed forces will rise up to desecrate the temple fortress and will abolish the daily sacrifice. Then they will set up the abomination that causes desolation.

Daniel 12:11

From the time that the daily sacrifice is abolished and the abomination that causes desolation is set up, there will be 1,290 days.

'FALSE PROPHETS'

2 Thessalonians 2:2–4

Do not become easily unsettled or alarmed by some prophecy . . . saying that the day of the Lord has already come. Don't let anyone deceive you in any way, for that day will not come, until the rebellion occurs and the man of lawlessness is revealed, the man doomed to destruction. He opposes and exalts himself over everything that is called God or is worshipped, and even sets himself up in God's temple, proclaiming himself to be God.

CHRISTIANS FLEE JERUSALEM

Eusebius, 'History of the Church', Book 3, Chapter 5

The members of the Jerusalem church, by means of a prophecy given by revelation to acceptable persons there, were ordered to leave the City before the war began and settle in a town in Peraea called Pella. To Pella those who believed in Christ migrated from Jerusalem.

"But in those days, following that distress,
'the sun will be darkened,
and the moon will not give its light;
the stars will fall from the sky,
and the heavenly bodies will be shaken.'
"At that time men will see the Son of Man
coming in clouds with great power and glory.
And he will send his angels and gather his
elect from the four winds, from the ends of
the earth to the ends of the heavens.

THE WRATH OF THE LORD

Isaiah 13:9–10,13

See, the day of the Lord is coming – a cruel day, with wrath and fierce anger – to make the land desolate and destroy the sinners within it. The stars of heaven and their constellations will not show their light. The rising sun will be darkened and the moon will not give its light. I will make the heavens tremble; and the earth will shake from its place at the wrath of the Lord Almighty, in the day of his burning anger.

Isaiah 34:2,4

The Lord is angry with all nations; his wrath is upon all their armies. He will totally destroy them, he will give them over to slaughter. All the stars of the heavens will be dissolved and the sky rolled up like a scroll; all the starry host will fall like withered leaves from the vine, like shrivelled figs from the fig-tree.

'SON OF MAN'

Daniel 7:13–14

In my vision at night I looked, and there before me was one like a son of man, coming with the clouds of heaven. He approached the Ancient of Days and was led into his presence. He was given authority, glory and sovereign power; all peoples, nations and men of every language worshipped him. His dominion is an everlasting dominion that will not pass away, and his kingdom is one that will never be destroyed.

'GATHER HIS ELECT'

Isaiah 11:10–12

In that day the Root of Jesse will stand as a banner for the peoples; the nations will rally to him, and his place of rest will be glorious. In that day the Lord will reach out his hand a second time to reclaim the remnant that is left of his people from Assyria, from Lower Egypt, from Upper Egypt, from Cush, from Elam, from Babylonia, from Hamath and from the islands of the sea. He will raise a banner for the nations and gather the exiles of Israel; he will assemble the scattered people of Judah from the four quarters of the earth.

Zechariah 2:6

"Come! Come! Flee from the land of the north," declares the Lord, "for I have scattered you to the four winds of heaven," declares the Lord.

"Now learn this lesson from the fig-tree: As soon as its twigs get tender and its leaves come out, you know that summer is near. Even so, when you see these things happening, you know that it is near, right at the door. I tell you the truth, this generation will certainly not pass away until all these things have happened. Heaven and earth will pass away, but my words will never pass away.

"No-one knows about that day or hour, not even the angels in heaven, nor the Son, but only the Father. Be on guard! Be alert! You do not know when that time will come. It's like a man going away: He leaves his house in charge of his servants, each with his assigned task, and tells the one at the door to keep watch.

"Therefore keep watch because you do not know when the owner of the house will come back—whether in the evening, or at midnight, or when the cock crows, or at dawn. If he comes suddenly, do not let him find you sleeping. What I say to you, I say to everyone: "Watch!" "

THE FUTURE

Isaiah 51:6

Lift up your eyes to the heavens, look at the earth beneath; the heavens will vanish like smoke, the earth will wear out like a garment and its inhabitants die like flies. But my salvation will last for ever, my righteousness will never fail.

THE EVERLASTING WORD

Isaiah 40:8

The grass withers and the flowers fall, but the word of our God stands for ever.

14

Now the Passover and the Feast of Unleavened Bread were only two days away, and the chief priests and the teachers of the law were looking for some sly way to arrest Jesus and kill him. "But not during the Feast," they said, "or the people may riot."

While he was in Bethany, reclining at the table in the home of a man known as Simon the Leper, a woman came with an alabaster jar of very expensive perfume, made of pure nard. She broke the jar and poured the perfume on his head.

Some of those present were saying indignantly to one another, "Why this waste of perfume? It could have been sold for more than a year's wages and the money given to the poor." And they rebuked her harshly.

"Leave her alone," said Jesus. "Why are you bothering her? She has done a beautiful thing to me. The poor you will always have with you, and you can help them any time you want. But you will not always have me. She did what she could. She poured perfume on my body beforehand to prepare for my burial. I tell you the truth, wherever the gospel is preached throughout the world, what she has done will also be told, in memory of her."

Then Judas Iscariot, one of the Twelve, went to the chief priests to betray Jesus to them. They were delighted to hear this and promised to give him money. So he watched for an opportunity to hand him over.

THE POOR ALWAYS WITH YOU

Deuteronomy 15:11

There will always be poor people in the land. Therefore I command you to be open-handed towards your brothers and towards the poor and needy in your land.

SAMUEL ANOINTS DAVID AS KING.

1 Samuel 16:12–13

The Lord said, "Rise and anoint him; he is the one." So Samuel took the horn of oil and anointed him in the presence of his brothers, and from that day on the Spirit of the Lord came upon David in power.

On the first day of the Feast of Unleavened Bread, when it was customary to sacrifice the Passover lamb, Jesus' disciples asked him, "Where do you want us to go and make preparations for you to eat the Passover?"

So he sent two of his disciples, telling them, "Go into the city, and a man carrying a pot of water will meet you. Follow him. Say to the owner of the house he enters, 'The Teacher asks: Where is my guest room, where I may eat the Passover with my disciples?' He will show you a large upper room, furnished and ready. Make preparations for us there."

The disciples left, went into the city and found things just as Jesus had told them. So they prepared the Passover.

PASSOVER REGULATIONS

Deuteronomy
16:1–3,5–7

Observe the month of Abib and celebrate the Passover of the Lord your God, because in the month of Abib he brought you out of Egypt by night. Sacrifice as the Passover to the Lord your God an animal from your flock or herd at the place the Lord will choose as a dwelling for his Name. Do not eat it with bread made with yeast, but for seven days eat unleavened bread, the bread of affliction,

because you left Egypt in haste – so that all the days of your life you may remember the time of your departure from Egypt . . . You must not sacrifice the Passover in any town the Lord your God gives you except in the place he will choose as a dwelling for his Name. There you must sacrifice the Passover in the evening, when the sun goes down, on the anniversary of your departure from Egypt. Roast it and eat it at the place the Lord your God will choose.

THE APOSTLE PAUL'S
TRADITION

1 Corinthians 11:23–26

For I received from the Lord what I also passed on to you: The Lord Jesus, on the night he was betrayed, took bread, and when he had given thanks, he broke it and said, "This is my body, which is for you; do this in remembrance of me." In the same way, after supper he took the cup, saying, "This cup is the new covenant in my blood; do this, whenever you drink it, in remembrance of me." For whenever you eat this bread and drink this cup, you proclaim the Lord's death until he comes.

THANKSGIVING OVER THE CUP

A Jewish Passover service

Blessed are you, O Lord our God, king of the universe, who feeds the whole world with goodness, with grace and with mercy. We thank you, O Lord our God, that you have caused us to inherit a goodly and pleasant land. Have mercy, O Lord our God, on Israel your people, and on Jerusalem your city, and on Zion the dwelling place of your glory, and upon your altar and upon your temple. Blessed are you, O Lord, you who build Jerusalem.

'EATING WITH ME'

Psalm 41:9

Even my close friend, whom I trusted, he who shared my bread, has lifted up his heel against me.

THE BLOOD OF THE COVENANT

Exodus 24:8

Moses then took the blood, sprinkled it on the people and said, "This is the blood of the covenant that the Lord has made with you in accordance with all these words."

'POURED OUT FOR MANY'

Isaiah 53:12

He poured out his life unto death . . . he bore the sins of many.

When evening came, Jesus arrived with the Twelve. While they were reclining at the table eating, he said, "I tell you the truth, one of you will betray me—one who is eating with me."

They were saddened, and one by one they said to him, "Surely not I?"

"It is one of the Twelve," he replied, "one who dips bread into the bowl with me. The Son of Man will go just as it is written about him. But woe to that man who betrays the Son of Man! It would be better for him if he had not been born."

While they were eating, Jesus took bread, gave thanks and broke it, and gave it to his disciples, saying, "Take it; this is my body."

Then he took the cup, gave thanks and offered it to them, and they all drank from it. "This is my blood of the covenant, which is poured out for many," he said to them. "I tell you the truth, I will not drink again of the fruit of the vine until that day when I drink it anew in the kingdom of God."

A NEW COVENANT

Jeremiah 31:31–34

"The time is coming," declares the Lord, "when I will make a new covenant with the house of Israel and with the house of Judah. It will not be like the covenant I made with their forefathers when I took them by the hand to lead them out of Egypt, because they broke my covenant, though I was a husband to them," declares the Lord.

"This is the covenant that I will make with the house of Israel after that time," declares the Lord. "I will put my law in their minds and write it on their hearts. I will be their God, and they will be my people. No longer will a man teach his neighbour, or a man his brother, saying, 'Know the Lord,' because they will all know me, from the least of them to the greatest," declares the Lord.

"For I will forgive their wickedness and will remember their sins no more."

A PSALM SUNG AT PASSOVER **Psalm 116**

I love the Lord, for he heard my voice; he heard my cry for mercy.
Because he turned his ear to me, I will call on him as long as I live.
The cords of death entangled me, the anguish of the grave came upon me;
    I was overcome by trouble and sorrow.
Then I called on the name of the Lord: ''O Lord, save me!''
The Lord is gracious and righteous; our God is full of compassion.
The Lord protects the simple-hearted; when I was in great need, he saved me.
Be at rest once more, O my soul, for the Lord has been good to you.
For you, O Lord, have delivered my soul from death, my eyes from tears, my
    feet from stumbling, that I may walk before the Lord in the land of the living.
I believed; therefore I said, ''I am greatly afflicted.''
And in my dismay I said, ''All men are liars.''
How can I repay the Lord for all his goodness to me?
I will lift up the cup of salvation and call on the name of the Lord.
I will fulfil my vows to the Lord in the presence of all his people.
Precious in the sight of the Lord is the death of his saints.
O Lord, truly I am your servant; I am your servant, the son of your
    maidservant; you have freed me from my chains.
I will sacrifice a thank-offering to you and call on the name of the Lord.
I will fulfil my vows to the Lord – in your midst, O Jerusalem.
Praise the Lord.

When they had sung a hymn, they went out to the Mount of Olives.

"You will all fall away," Jesus told them, "for it is written:

'I will strike the shepherd,
    and the sheep will be scattered.'

But after I have risen, I will go ahead of you into Galilee."

Peter declared, "Even if all fall away, I will not."

"I tell you the truth," Jesus answered, "today—yes, tonight—before the cock crows twice you yourself will disown me three times."

But Peter insisted emphatically, "Even if I have to die with you, I will never disown you." And all the others said the same."

'STRIKE THE SHEPHERD' **Zechariah 13:7**

''Awake, O sword, against my shepherd, against the man who is close to me!''
declares the Lord Almighty. ''Strike the shepherd, and the sheep will be
scattered, and I will turn my hand against the little ones.''

They went to a place called Gethsemane, and Jesus said to his disciples, "Sit here while I pray." He took Peter, James and John along with him, and he began to be deeply distressed and troubled. "My soul is overwhelmed with sorrow to the point of death," he said to them. "Stay here and keep watch."

Going a little farther, he fell to the ground and prayed that if possible the hour might pass from him. "Abba, Father," he said, "everything is possible for you. Take this cup from me. Yet not what I will, but what you will."

Then he returned to his disciples and found them sleeping. "Simon," he said to Peter, "are you asleep? Could you not keep watch for one hour? Watch and pray so that you will not fall into temptation. The spirit is willing, but the body is weak."

Once more he went away and prayed the same thing. When he came back, he again found them sleeping, because their eyes were heavy. They did not know what to say to him.

Returning the third time, he said to them, "Are you still sleeping and resting? Enough! The hour has come. Look, the Son of Man is betrayed into the hands of sinners. Rise! Let us go! Here comes my betrayer!"

'MY SOUL IS OVERWHELMED'

Psalm 22:20–21

Deliver my life from the sword, my precious life from the power of the dogs. Rescue me from the mouth of the lions.

Psalm 31:9–10

Be merciful to me, O Lord, for I am in distress; my eyes grow weak with sorrow, my soul and my body with grief. My life is consumed by anguish, and my years by groaning.

Psalm 42:5–6

Why are you downcast, O my soul? Why so disturbed within me? Put your hope in God, for I will yet praise him, my Saviour and my God.

THE LORD'S PRAYER

Matthew 6:9–13

Father . . . your kingdom come, your will be done . . . do not put us to the test, but save us from evil.

'THE CUP'

Habbakuk 2:16

Now it is your turn! Drink and be exposed! The cup from the Lord's right hand is coming round to you, and disgrace will cover your glory.

Just as he was speaking, Judas, one of the Twelve, appeared. With him was a crowd armed with swords and clubs, sent from the chief priests, the teachers of the law and the elders.

Now the betrayer had arranged a signal with them: "The one I kiss is the man; arrest him and lead him away under guard." Going at once to Jesus, Judas said, "Rabbi!" and kissed him. The men seized Jesus and arrested him. Then one of those standing near drew his sword and struck the servant of the high priest, cutting off his ear.

"Am I leading a rebellion," said Jesus, "that you have come out with swords and clubs to capture me? Every day I was with you, teaching in the temple courts, and you did not arrest me. But the Scriptures must be fulfilled." Then everyone deserted him and fled.

A young man, wearing nothing but a linen garment, was following Jesus. When they seized him, he fled naked, leaving his garment behind.

'KISS'

Proverbs 27:6

The kisses of an enemy may be profuse, but faithful are the wounds of a friend.

'FLED NAKED'

Amos 2:16

"Even the bravest warriors will flee naked on that day," declares the Lord.

They took Jesus to the high priest, and all the chief priests, elders and teachers of the law came together. Peter followed him at a distance, right into the courtyard of the high priest. There he sat with the guards and warmed himself at the fire.

The chief priests and the whole Sanhedrin were looking for evidence against Jesus so that they could put him to death, but they did not find any. Many testified falsely against him, but their statements did not agree.

Then some stood up and gave this false testimony against him: "We heard him say, 'I will destroy this man-made temple and in three days will build another, not made by man.'" Yet even then their testimony did not agree.

Then the high priest stood up before them and asked Jesus, "Are you not going to answer? What is this testimony that these men are bringing against you? But Jesus remained silent and gave no answer.

Again the high priest asked him, "Are you the Christ, the Son of the Blessed One?"

"I am," said Jesus. "And you will see the Son of Man sitting at the right hand of the Mighty One and coming on the clouds of heaven."

The high priest tore his clothes. "Why do we need any more witnesses?" he asked. "You have heard the blasphemy. What do you think?"

They all condemned him as worthy of death. Then some began to spit at him; they blindfolded him, struck him with their fists, and said, "Prophesy!" And the guards took him and beat him.

WITNESSES

Deuteronomy 19:15

One witness is not enough to convict a man accused of any crime or offence he may have committed. A matter must be established by the testimony of two or three witnesses.

'TESTIFIED FALSELY'

Psalm 27:12

Do not hand me over to the desire of my foes, for false witnesses rise up against me, breathing out violence.

'SITTING AT THE RIGHT HAND'

Psalm 110:1

The Lord says to my Lord: "Sit at my right hand until I make your enemies a footstool for your feet."

'SILENT AND GAVE NO ANSWER'

Psalm 38:12–14

Those who seek my life set their traps, those who would harm me talk of my ruin; all day long they plot deception. I am like a deaf man, who cannot hear, like a mute, who cannot open his mouth; I have become like a man who does not hear, whose mouth can offer no reply.

LAW ON BLASPHEMY

Leviticus 24:13–16

Take the blasphemer outside the camp. All those who heard him are to lay their hands on his head, and the entire assembly is to stone him. Say to the Israelites: "If anyone curses his God, he will be held responsible; anyone who has blasphemed the name of the Lord must be put to death. The entire assembly must stone him."

'SPAT AT HIM . . . AND BEAT HIM'

Isaiah 50:6

I offered my back to those who beat me, my cheeks to those who pulled out my beard; I did not hide my face from mocking and spitting.

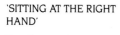

While Peter was below in the courtyard, one of the servant girls of the high priest came by. When she saw Peter warming himself, she looked closely at him.

"You also were with that Nazarene, Jesus," she said.

But he denied it. "I don't know or understand what you're talking about," he said, and went out into the entrance.

When the servant girl saw him there, she said again to those standing around, "This fellow is one of them." Again he denied it.

After a little while, those standing near said to Peter, "Surely you are one of them, for you are a Galilean."

He began to call down curses on himself, and he swore to them, "I don't know this man you're talking about."

Immediately the cock crowed the second time. Then Peter remembered the word Jesus had spoken to him: "Before the rooster crows twice you will disown me three times." And he broke down and wept.

Psalm 38:11

My friends and companions avoid me because of my wounds; my neighbours stay far away.

15

JOSEPHUS REFERS TO JESUS

Antiquities 18:63–64

About this time there lived Jesus, a wise man. For he was one who performed surprising works, and a teacher of people who with pleasure received the unusual. He stirred up many Jews and also many of the Greeks. But when Pilate condemned him to the cross (since he was accused by men of the highest standing among us) those who had been loving him from the first did not cease to cause trouble. And the tribe of Christians, named after him, has still to this day not disappeared.

Very early in the morning, the chief priests, with the elders, the teachers of the law and the whole Sanhedrin, reached a decision. They bound Jesus, led him away and turned him over to Pilate.

"Are you the king of the Jews?" asked Pilate.

"The words are yours," Jesus replied. The chief priests accused him of many things. So again Pilate asked him, "Aren't you going to answer? See how many things they are accusing you of."

But Jesus still made no reply, and Pilate was amazed.

Now it was the custom at the Feast to release a prisoner whom the people requested. A man called Barabbas was in prison with the insurrectionists who had committed murder in the uprising. The crowd came up and asked Pilate to do for them what he usually did.

"Do you want me to release to you the king of the Jews?" asked Pilate, knowing it was out of envy that the chief priests had handed Jesus over to him. But the chief priests stirred up the crowd to have Pilate release Barabbas instead.

"What shall I do, then, with the one you call the king of the Jews?" Pilate asked them.

"Crucify him!" they shouted.

"Why? What crime has he committed?" asked Pilate.

But they shouted all the louder, "Crucify him!"

Wanting to satisfy the crowd, Pilate released Barabbas to them. He had Jesus flogged, and handed him over to be crucified.

'NO REPLY'

Isaiah 53:5,7

He was pierced for our transgressions, he was crushed for our iniquities; the punishment that brought us peace was upon him, and by his wounds we are healed . . . He was oppressed and afflicted, yet he did not open his mouth.

'FLOGGED'

Isaiah 50:6

I offered my back to those who beat me.

The soldiers led Jesus away into the palace (that is, the Praetorium) and called together the whole company of soldiers. They put a purple robe on him, then wove a crown of thorns and set it on him. And they began to call out to him, "Hail, King of the Jews!" Again and again they struck him on the head with a staff and spat on him. Falling on their knees, they worshipped him. And when they had mocked him, they took off the purple robe and put his own clothes on him. Then they led him out to crucify him.

'MOCKING AND SPITTING'

Isaiah 50:6

I did not hide my face from mocking and spitting.

'DESPISED AND REJECTED'

Isaiah 53:3

He was despised and rejected by men.

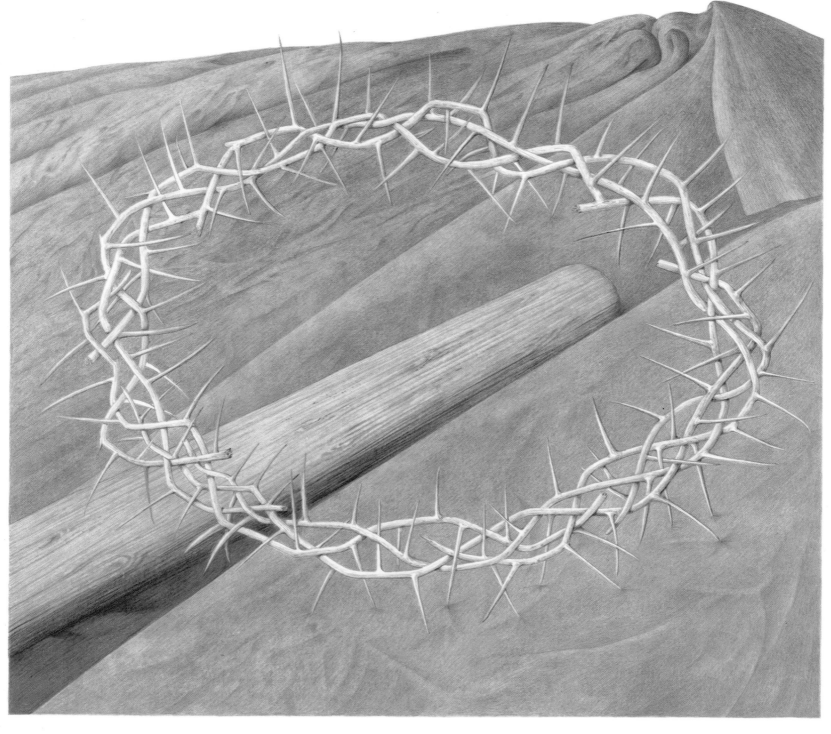

A certain man from Cyrene, Simon, the father of Alexander and Rufus, was passing by on his way in from the country, and they forced him to carry the cross. They brought Jesus to the place called Golgotha (which means The Place of the Skull). Then they offered him wine mixed with myrrh, but he did not take it. And they crucified him. Dividing up his clothes, they cast lots to see what each would get.

It was the third hour when they crucified him. The written notice of the charge against him read: THE KING OF THE JEWS. They crucified two robbers with him, one on his right and one on his left. Those who passed by hurled insults at him, shaking their heads and saying, "So! You who are going to destroy the temple and build it in three days, come down from the cross and save yourself!"

In the same way the chief priests and the teachers of the law mocked him among themselves. "He saved others," they said, "but he can't save himself! Let this Christ, this King of Israel, come down now from the cross, that we may see and believe." Those crucified with him also heaped insults on him.

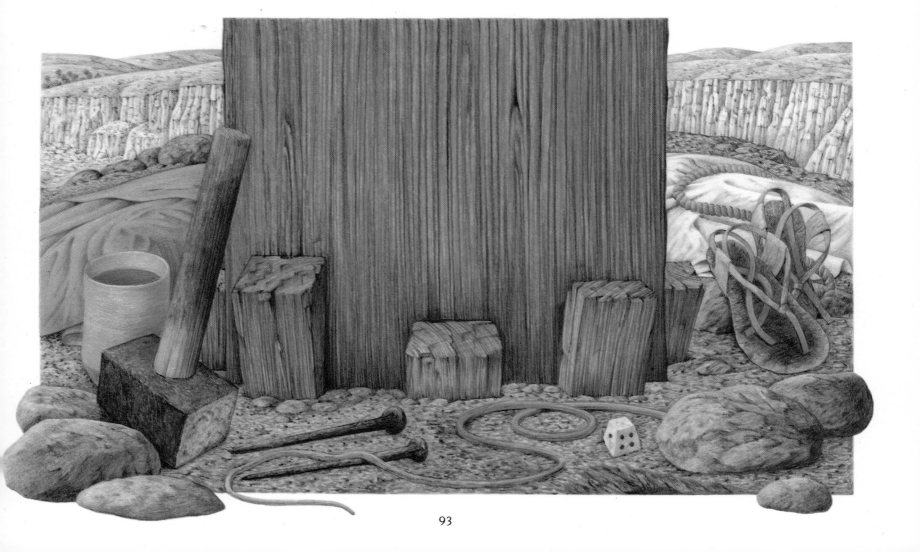

MIDDAY DARKNESS

Amos 8:9

''In that day,'' declares the
Sovereign Lord,
''I will make the sun go
down at noon and darken
the earth in broad
daylight.''

'VINEGAR'

Psalm 69:21

They put gall in my food
and gave me vinegar for
my thirst.

'CURTAIN OF THE TEMPLE'

Exodus 26:31,33

Make a curtain of blue,
purple and scarlet yarn
and finely twisted linen,
with cherubim worked into
it by a skilled
craftsman . . . Hang the
curtain from the clasps
and place the ark of the
Testimony behind the
curtain. The curtain will
separate the Holy Place
from the Most Holy Place.

At the sixth hour darkness came over the whole land until the ninth hour. And at the ninth hour Jesus cried out in a loud voice, "Eloi, Eloi, lama sabachthani?"— which means, "My God, my God, why have you forsaken me?"

When some of those standing near heard this, they said, "Listen, he's calling Elijah." One man ran, filled a sponge with wine vinegar, put it on a stick, and offered it to Jesus to drink. "Leave him alone now. Let's see if Elijah comes to take him down," he said.

With a loud cry, Jesus breathed his last. The curtain of the temple was torn in two from top to bottom. And when the centurion, who stood there in front of Jesus, heard his cry and saw how he died, he said, "Surely this man was a son of God!"

Some women were watching from a distance. Among them were Mary Magdalene, Mary the mother of James the younger and of Joses, and Salome. In Galilee these women had followed him and cared for his needs. Many other women who had come up with him to Jerusalem were also there.

SUFFERING PREDICTED

Psalm 22:1,2,15,27

My God, my God, why
have you forsaken me?
Why are you so far from
saving me, so far from my
groaning?

'DARKNESS'

O my God, I cry out by
day, but you do not
answer, by night, and am
not silent.

'THIRST'

My strength is dried up
like a potsherd, and my
tongue sticks to the roof
of my mouth; you lay me
in the dust of death.

'THE CENTURION'

All the ends of the earth
will remember and turn to
the Lord, and all the
families of the nations will
bow down before him.

BURIAL OF A HANGED
CORPSE

**Deuteronomy
21:22–23**

If a man guilty of a capital
offence is put to death
and his body is hung on a
tree, you must not leave
his body on the tree
overnight. Be sure to bury
him that same day,
because anyone who is
hung on the tree is under
God's curse. You must not
desecrate the land the
Lord your God is giving
you as an inheritance.

It was Preparation Day (that is, the day before the Sabbath). So as evening approached, Joseph of Arimathea, a prominent member of the Council who was himself waiting for the kingdom of God went boldly to Pilate and asked for Jesus' body. Pilate was surprised to hear that he was already dead. Summoning the centurion, he asked him if Jesus had already died. When he learned from the centurion that it was so, he gave the body to Joseph. So Joseph brought some linen cloth, took down the body, wrapped it in the linen, and placed it in a tomb cut out of rock. Then he rolled a stone against the entrance of the tomb. Mary Magdalene and Mary the mother of Joses saw where he was laid.

CARRION

**Juvenal, Satires
14:77f**

The vulture hurries from
dead cattle and dogs and
crosses, to bring some of
the carrion to her
offspring.

'A GRAVE WITH THE RICH'

Isaiah 53:9

He was assigned a grave
with the wicked, and with
the rich in his death,
though he had done no
violence, nor was any
deceit in his mouth.

16

When the Sabbath was over, Mary Magdalene, Mary the mother of James, and Salome bought spices so that they might go to anoint Jesus' body. Very early on the first day of the week, just after sunrise, they were on their way to the tomb and they asked each other, "Who will roll the stone away from the entrance of the tomb?"

But when they looked up, they saw that the stone, which was very large, had been rolled away. As they entered the tomb, they saw a young man dressed in a white robe sitting on the right side, and they were alarmed.

"Don't be alarmed," he said. "You are looking for Jesus the Nazarene, who was crucified. He has risen! He is not here. See the place where they laid him. But go, tell his disciples and Peter, 'He is going ahead of you into Galilee. There you will see him, just as he told you.' "

Trembling and bewildered, the women went out and fled from the tomb. They said nothing to anyone, because they were afraid.

Notes to the text and illustrations

THE WORLD OF JESUS

Mark's Gospel comes to us from a time and a culture very different from the present-day world—so different, in fact, that a modern reader will inevitably miss a host of allusions without the aid of accompanying comments. In particular, the Gospel text makes little sense without some background knowledge of the culture of the time, the intentions of the Gospel writer, and the methods he employed. The next three pages are by way of a brief introduction, to give some background information and to provide a helpful way in to understanding this fascinating Gospel.

The action described in the Gospel takes place within a very limited region of the eastern Mediterranean coastlands. From the northernmost town mentioned (Tyre) to the southernmost (Jerusalem) is a distance of barely 125 miles/200 kms. Many of the stories recounted in the early part of the book are placed in a single small area around the Sea of Galilee (or Lake Tiberias, as it is now known). This is an inland lake about 12.5 miles/20 kms across at its widest point. It was famous for its fishing, and for a very fertile strip of land along its north-west shore. The whole region was very thickly populated in Jesus' day, and it had lively commercial activity, because important trade routes crossed it. Jesus' main base seems to have been Capernaum on the northern shore of the lake.

However, some stories show him travelling around neighbouring territories, including Phoenician Tyre (in present-day Lebanon), and the district to the east of Galilee called Decapolis (present-day Syria and Jordan). The population of these territories was predominantly gentile (that is, non-Jewish).

By contrast, all the action in the second half of the book takes place further south, in or around Jerusalem. This had been the ancient capital city of King David over a thousand years earlier, and in this city King Solomon had built a great Temple to Yahweh, the Hebrew God. The successor to that Temple was the focal point of what was in Jesus' day a very large walled city—with a population of perhaps 40,000 people.

In the time of Jesus, the whole of this region was under strong Roman influence. But it was not yet a single province of the empire. To travel from Galilee to Jerusalem one had to cross several borders. Galilee was ruled by a puppet king (or 'tetrarch') called Herod Antipas. The population of his domain was Jewish, and proudly independent from the Judean Jews of the Jerusalem area.

Judea was more closely ruled by the Romans from their newly founded seaport capital of Caesarea. The Roman official governing Judea in Jesus' time was Pontius Pilatus, who was 'prefect of Judea' from 26 to 36CE. Contemporary historical sources show him to have been a cruel and intemperate man, who was eventually removed from office by the Emperor.

Throughout the area, the Romans had imposed taxes, which crippled the poor and caused huge resentment. The political situation was thus highly volatile. On the one hand, the powerful priesthood of the Jerusalem Temple had come to a compromise arrangement with the Roman forces, and were in return permitted to carry on their monotheistic religion without interference. But on the other hand, many Jewish nationalists thought that their leaders had betrayed them, and took to the hills in armed guerrilla warfare, vainly hoping to expel the Roman forces.

So the setting in which Jesus lived was politically very unstable. After his life-time, things progressively deteriorated until eventually (in 67CE), they exploded in a full-scale rebellion of bloody proportions. Jewish resistance was heroic, but in the end futile in the face of Rome's professional army. A last stand was taken within the Temple itself, but after a lengthy siege it was captured, burned, and razed to the ground in 70CE.

Jesus was thus living in a critical period of Jewish history. Jerusalem's priestly leaders were on the lookout for nationalistic extremists who might upset the uneasy compromise they had established with the Romans. With all the popular talk about him being 'God's anointed', Jesus inevitably aroused suspicion, which led to official action to suppress him, and eventually eliminate him.

Jesus lived within a highly developed culture, in a country criss-crossed by a good road system. Galilee itself was a kind of cross-roads in the major trade-routes of the east, so much wealth was generated through commerce. While life in villages might be materially poor, those who lived in towns and cities could become fabulously rich. Archaeologists have unearthed the houses of Jerusalem aristocrats: they were large stone-built villas with mosaic floors, carved stone tables, and elaborate designs painted on the wall plaster. On the other hand, rural inhabitants often had to 'make do'. A recent exciting archaeological find from Galilee was the hull of a fishing boat preserved in the mud of the lake bed. Scientific examination of its timbers indicate is was in use during the first century CE, that it had been repaired many times (sometimes with rather inadequate pieces of wood), and had been in consistent use for about a century.

Because of the multi-racial composition of the area's population, many languages will have been spoken. Aramaic was the common language of the indigenous population, and it was undoubtedly Jesus' mother tongue. Several Aramaic sayings of his are preserved in the Gospel text. But Hebrew, a sister language to Aramaic, will also have been spoken in religious contexts. This was the ancient language of the Jews, whose scriptures were written in it. Jesus undoubtedly understood Hebrew, and could read it in the synagogue scrolls, when called upon to do so. He may also have understood Greek, the language spoken in the Greek cities of Decapolis. He chose as a disciple a man with a Greek name (Philip), who will probably have been brought up in a Greek-speaking household. Latin, too, will have been heard in the streets, or at least wherever Roman soldiers were present. Several Latin words occur in the Gospel: for example, *denarius* (the name of a coin), and *praetorium* (the name of the governor's palace). So life, especially in the cities, had a pretty cosmopolitan tone about it.

One of the least attractive aspects of Roman culture was their custom of executing by crucifixion those convicted of treason against the state. The condemned man was nailed or tied to a heavy vertical wooden stake, jointed to a horizontal cross-piece. The criminal was left to hang naked, exposed to the elements and to public abuse, until he died. Death might not occur for several days. The whole intention of the spectacle was to act as a public deterrent to would-be rebels.

Throughout the Gospel, a wide range of Jewish religious customs are mentioned without explanation: knowledge of them was taken for granted in the original readers. The Sabbath, for example, was the name of the seventh day of the week (Saturday) on which pious Jews refrained from work in accordance with the laws laid out in the Jewish scriptures. The actual definition of 'work' was a matter which was hotly debated between those who held a lenient and those who held a stricter interpretation of the law. Jesus found himself embroiled in this debate.

A similar issue was the elaborate customs surrounding food and the vessels it was served in. Religious law classified certain foods (such as pork) as 'unclean'; food or vessels could become 'unclean' by being in contact with a dead body, or a menstruating woman. Pious Jews tried to avoid any contact with 'unclean' items.

The foundation of all Jewish religion was the scriptures. These were a group of writings (usually referred to by Christians as 'the Old Testament') which had been collected over the centuries, and had acquired the status of sacred scripture. The scriptures were of several kinds: the oldest portion, called 'the Law', was thought to have been written by Moses; then came collections of prophetic writings; and finally a later collection of miscellaneous writings, including the Psalms (hymns designed to be sung during Temple rituals). By the time of Jesus these scriptures had taken on a more or less fixed form, and were the essential basis for all religious discussion and argument. They were written on leather scrolls, and every Jewish boy was trained to read them.

Educated Jews would know large portions of the scriptures off by heart. Their knowledge was continually reinforced at formal gatherings in the synagogue. Every Jewish community had its local synagogue (or assembly room) which was used both for study and for corporate public worship. At these meetings, held weekly on the

Sabbath, the scriptures would be read out aloud, following a scheme which ensured that the whole of the Law was systematically worked through.

Very different was the public worship in the Temple at Jerusalem. Here the worship centred around the sacrifice of animals and crops. This meant that worshippers brought the appropriate offering (different offerings were specified in the law for different purposes—as thanksgiving at the birth of a child, for example, or to atone for a wrongdoing). A priest would receive the offering at a huge stone altar built in the open air; a portion of the offering would be burned on the altar, and was regarded as being given to God. All of this took place within a series of vast open courtyards, surrounded by the most sumptuous architecture of its day. When Jesus was alive, the finishing touches were still being put to this great complex of buildings, begun a generation beforehand by King Herod the Great. So monumental was the scale of these buildings that, had they survived the destruction of 70CE, they would probably have come to be regarded as one of the Wonders of the World.

The open courts of the Temple were designed to hold enormous crowds of Jewish people who would come from all over the ancient world on pilgrimage at the great festivals of the year, such as the Feast of Passover. This was the annual occasion in March/April when the Jewish people commemorated their miraculous escape from slavery in Egypt over a thousand years before. The worship on these occasions would be spectacular, with colourful processions, choirs singing, bands of musical instruments, priests arrayed in special vestments, and ritual vessels of solid gold glistening in the sun. Little wonder that the Temple was considered the visible sign of God's presence with his people. And little wonder that when Jesus spoke critically of it, he provoked deep and angry opposition.

Jewish religion of the time was by no means uniform, and a variety of different religious movements were flourishing alongside each other. The Pharisees, for example, were a group aiming to live in ordinary society, while strictly observing the regulations commanded in the Law. Despite the impression given in this Gospel, they were good, earnest, spiritually minded people, seeking to live a disciplined lifestyle. However, they clashed with Jesus over his more lenient interpretation of religious law.

The priesthood of the Jerusalem Temple was perhaps the most powerful group of religious leaders, since they had control of the great Temple, and all the influence it exerted. Moreover, the Sanhedrin, the supreme religious council, sat in the Temple precincts and was presided over by the High Priest. By challenging the Temple authorities, Jesus was doing something little short of challenging the government of a state—for in the ancient world the present-day distinction between sacred and secular did not exist.

Apart from the Gospels themselves, what other historical evidence survives about Jesus? Virtually nothing. But there are some contemporary documents which help historians build up a general picture of the period.

The most significant source of external evidence is the work of the Jewish historian Flavius Josephus. He lived just after the time of Jesus, from 38 to 100CE, and wrote two lengthy books—*The Jewish War* (an eyewitness account of the unsuccessful war of Jewish independence, 66-70CE) and *Antiquities of the Jews* (a history of the Jewish people from the beginning until his own day). Josephus had lived in Galilee, which he describes in much detail; he was also a priest, and was able to give extensive accounts of the Temple's architecture from personal knowledge. He wrote within a few years of Mark's Gospel being compiled, and his evidence is amongst the most important now surviving regarding Palestine and Jewish culture in the time of Jesus. In one brief paragraph he actually mentions Jesus by name—the only contemporary non-biblical source to do so. The passage (in *Antiquities* 18:63-64) has been tampered with by later Christian scribes to make it appear that Josephus spoke of Jesus as the Christ. But scholars are generally agreed that if the Christian additions are removed from the text, what Josephus probably wrote was this:

'About this time there lived Jesus, a wise man. For he was one who performed surprising works, and a teacher of people who with pleasure receive the unusual. He stirred up many Jews and also many of the Greeks. And when Pilate condemned him to the cross, since he was accused by men of the highest standing amongst us, those who had been loving him from the first did not cease to cause trouble. And until now the tribe of Christians, so named from him, is not yet extinct.'

All of this sounds perfectly authentic from a Jew who had no special interest in the tiny sect called 'Christians'. It is significant that Jesus was remembered in Josephus' circles as a 'wise man', a healer and teacher, condemned to crucifixion under Pilate—corroboration of the kernel of the Gospel story.

Other sources of indirect information are remarks about Roman culture in classical Roman writers such as Seneca, Quintilian and Juvenal—all of whom describe the revulsion they felt about crucifixions. A further source is the early Christian writer Justin Martyr, a native of Palestine, who in his writings sometimes refers to traditions about Jesus which were circulating orally amongst the Jewish-Christians of Palestine in about 160CE.

There is one other kind of evidence which helps to inform our present-day understanding of the Gospel story. In recent years, archaeologists have discovered surprising material associated with sites mentioned in the Gospel. At Capernaum, a house-church apparently built over the site of Peter's home; in the mud near Magdala, a fishing boat which sailed the lake in Jesus' day; in Jerusalem, remains of the monumental foundations of Herod's great Temple; at Golgotha, the lie of the land at the site of the crucifixion. Rex Nicholls' illustrations give visual expression to some of what scholars have found out about these things.

Taken as a whole, these external sources of evidence show that the Gospel story fits comfortably into a historical setting which can now be verified independently.

INTERPRETING MARK'S GOSPEL

A quick reading of Mark's Gospel shows it to be a rather peculiar composition. While in some respects like a biography, it lacks many characteristics which one might expect in such a work. It clearly has a central figure (Jesus of Nazareth), and the book is almost entirely taken up with describing small incidents in his life and some of his sayings, together with a very detailed account of the last three days of his life. But there is no attempt to offer the reader any account of Jesus' appearance, family background, or personal characteristics; neither does the writer try to suggest what motivated Jesus' behaviour, or where he got his ideas from. One might expect that an author of a biography would attempt to concentrate on the personality of his subject. But none of this is present in this book. So we must draw the conclusion that it is a mistake to read the book as though it is a biography.

Comparisons with other literature of the time make it plain that this book was breaking new ground. It was a new kind of literature. This becomes plain in the author's chosen title for his work. He did not call his book 'The Life of Jesus', but 'The Gospel of Jesus'. This word had never before been applied to a book; 'gospel' was a specifically Christian jargon word for the series of things that Christians proclaimed about Jesus. So the title helps us to see the author's intention: he considered he was producing a written-down version of Christian belief about Jesus—rather a different undertaking from writing a biography. So the very use of the word 'gospel' to describe the work tells us quite a bit about the author's intentions, as we shall see later.

But first, there is a particular problem that modern readers have. The New Testament contains three other Gospels, now bearing the names of Matthew, Luke and John. Modern readers who know these other Gospels can all too easily carry over information from them into their reading of Mark's Gospel; whereas Mark's Gospel was, of course, originally intended to make full sense by itself. So if we are to respond to it in the same way as its original readers, we shall need to try and come to it as if it were the first gospel we have ever encountered.

If we do this, we are likely to be struck by the picture of Jesus which is presented in Mark's Gospel. He comes on the scene out of the blue: there is no account of his birth or family or up-bringing, and none of the political or historical setting of his life. The book seems to be made up of rather disjointed little paragraphs, and it is difficult to trace much development of events. The stories are mostly about healings (and also some strange wonders—such as a storm being stilled by a word of command). There are also snippets of Jesus' sayings and a few memorable stories that he used to illustrate his teachings. But we are not given any systematic impression of 'the teaching of Jesus'. It clearly was not the author's intention to do any such thing.

However, at chapter 14, everything changes. At this point a connected narrative takes over, quite different in style from what has preceded. The snippets and disjointed paragraphs disappear, and instead we are offered a consecutive account of Jesus' last day of freedom, his arrest, detention in custody, trial, execution and burial. The narrative ends with an account of how visiting mourners failed to find the body two days later. Clearly these final episodes to Jesus' story were very important to the author, or he would not have devoted so much space to them.

All of this is apparently what the author regarded as 'the Gospel of Jesus'. We must suppose that there is an inner coherence to it, even though that may not be immediately apparent to modern readers. To find its coherence we need to understand the thought-world of the first readers. Fortunately, recent scholarship has done much to help modern readers reconstruct it. If we can mentally enter into that world, we can discern a coherence in the Gospel which might otherwise escape us.

A key idea is contained in the phrase 'the kingdom of God', which occurs frequently in the preserved words of Jesus. His initial proclamation was 'The kingdom of God is near'. What may the first readers have understood by this? They will have presumed that its meaning was spiritual, although the imagery employed is political and military. Their assumptions were something like this: God is Lord or King of the universe; he created it and he controls the events that happen within it; nevertheless, there is an evil force temporarily tyrannizing the world; this evil force shows itself through sicknesses which afflict people, or through demons who possess people, through other destructive powers such as storms, and most particularly through death. There was a belief that this evil tyranny was only temporary, and that a time would come when, in a great cosmic battle, God would finally defeat the powers of evil. Then 'the kingdom of God' would be established. Precisely what kind of existence this would be was a bit hazy, but social justice and physical health and international peace were certainly a part of it. It was commonly spoken of as a new age which would be like a huge banquet with God as the host.

Given these assumptions about the world, Mark's Gospel immediately appears to be making an enormous claim. It is claiming that the moment of the great cosmic battle is virtually upon us; the powers of evil have already been challenged, and they are losing ground; the signs of the coming of the kingdom of God are evident for anyone with eyes to see. It is all happening (the Gospel claims) through Jesus, through whom God is acting to defeat the tyranny of evil: Jesus is driving back the domain of Satan as he heals the sick, exorcizes demons, raises the dead, stills a storm, and challenges the authority of corrupt political and religious leaders. He even seems to be anticipating the heavenly banquet by miraculously feeding vast crowds of followers. Thus the apparently peculiar selection of stories may be seen to have a clear coherence, once the assumptions of the time are understood.

Another key idea concerns the ancient Hebrew scriptures, which were assumed to be a special revelation from God to humanity. At their centre was the extended account of how God had intervened in history to rescue Israel from slavery in Egypt, and how he had sent Moses to lead them; how the Egyptian oppressors had been smitten with plagues, and Israel had escaped; how they miraculously crossed the Sea of Reeds, which drowned the Egyptian army; how they were miraculously fed with both meat and bread in the desert beyond the Sea; how they were eventually led by Moses' successor Joshua into the Promised Land; and how over succeeding centuries God had sent prophets such as Elijah to Israel to keep them faithful. All Jewish people had these stories in their blood; they believed in a God who acted in history to deliver his people from oppression.

Given this knowledge, and this set of ideas, the claim that Mark's Gospel is making about Jesus appears to be greatly strengthened. Jesus is presented as a second Moses and a second Elijah (both of whom appear to him in the visionary experience of the transfiguration); like Moses, he delivers the sick from plagues, he takes the disciples safely across the Sea of Galilee, and miraculously feeds the people in a desert place on the other side. At the Last Supper, he deliberately links his impending death with the Passover, implying that through his death God will achieve a deliverance like that earlier deliverance from slavery in Egypt.

This Gospel's writer considered that Jesus' death was the moment which ushered in the New Age. That is why he devotes such lengthy attention to the Passion Narrative (as chapters 14 to 16 are sometimes called), and why the book ends in such an astonishing way. If the New Age has indeed begun, if death has actually been overcome, that is almost beyond our comprehension, and certainly beyond words. So, like many modern novels, the Gospel ends inconclusively, requiring readers to draw their own conclusions.

THE AUTHOR AND HIS READERS

Who were these first readers? The work contains no dedication, neither is any individual or group specifically addressed. But by paying careful attention to the details of how some things are explained, it is possible to get a rough impression of the intended audience.

They appear to be Christians who already have some knowledge of the events surrounding Jesus, and also a good knowledge of the Jewish scriptures. They speak Greek, and need Aramaic words explained to them. They seem to be living at a place and time when they are being persecuted for their Christian faith, and having to answer for themselves in law-courts. If some of them were once conscientious members of Jewish synagogues, that is no longer the case—they have been expelled from membership. Indeed they do not seem to be living in a fully Jewish setting at all, for their customs about divorce are Roman rather than Jewish. Some readers seem to be gentiles, for they need some Jewish customs explained. They now belong to a Christian sub-culture, which has already evolved its own technical terms, such as 'the gospel', 'the word', or 'the Christ'. Some of their members have begun to fall away, through fear of persecution, or simply for love of more material values.

The text itself is anonymous: the author makes no allusion to himself at all. So there is really no means of knowing who the author was, or where he was living. For that reason, the commentary that follows will refer simply to 'the author' or 'the evangelist'. (In our modern Bibles, the text carries the title 'The Gospel according to Mark', but that wording is no part of the original document; it simply reflects an early-second-century belief that someone called Mark was the writer. However, since Marcus was the commonest of Latin names in the Roman empire, we are not much further forward.)

But if we cannot determine the author's name or location (because of his deliberate anonymity), there are many indications from his writing about his interests, beliefs, and methods.

His prime concern was to present known traditions about Jesus in a form that communicated itself to his audience—whom we may reasonably suppose was the community of Christians living in his own city or region. He will have been writing for people whose problems he well knew; in particular he knew the immediate difficulties they were having in holding on to their Christian faith, and in presenting it to their neighbours.

One of these problems was the inconvenient fact that although Christians claimed Jesus was 'the Son of God', it was indisputable that he had died by crucifixion, a method of execution reserved for criminals and traitors against Rome. How did it come about that God's chosen 'anointed one', 'the Christ', came to such a disgraceful end? Unless this question could be adequately answered, there was little prospect of Roman citizens (or indeed anyone else) becoming

Christians. So a major emphasis of the Gospel story is to show that it was God's will that Jesus should suffer, and that he did so innocently, and not because of any crime against the state.

Another practical problem facing his audience was the matter of suffering. Why was it that God was not protecting them from suffering as Christians? The author uses the theme of discipleship to explore this problem. He takes the example of Peter, and shows how in many stories it is clear that Peter expected God to intervene miraculously to save both Jesus and his followers from suffering. Jesus, however, is consistently shown as believing that the way of suffering was divinely ordained for him, and that his disciples must expect no less. However, Peter and the others never seem fully to grasp the meaning of this. Indeed the author seems to suggest that although they were closest to Jesus, the disciples were quite 'blind' to some of the things that were happening before their very eyes; only very slowly did they come to 'see' the meaning of what Jesus was showing them. The evangelist seems to imply that the inner meaning of Christian faith is not obvious to everyone, and that light may only dawn slowly for an individual over a period of time.

The way in which the evangelist speaks of all this is indirect and quite subtle. He does it through the skilful way in which he goes about his editorial work, selecting particular little stories or groups of sayings from the tradition, and then arranging them in a particular order and pattern. It is as though he has inherited a collection of precious beads of differing colours and materials; but they are loose and unstrung, and his task is to string them together; he is free to create a pattern with the beads. Some of the patterns he has organized are discussed in the commentary, particularly those with the themes of discipleship, suffering and blindness.

So the evangelist's task was really that of an editor. He had not been an eye-witness of the events described, so what he has written did not come straight out of his head as a piece of creative writing. Rather he had available to him a rich store of stories about Jesus which had been preserved by the Christian community through oral tradition. That is to say, from the beginning people had told stories about Jesus, and had repeated his sayings. In the process of constant repetition, these stories had taken on a fixed shape, and the sayings had been memorized because their teaching was considered very important.

It seems that Mark's Gospel is constructed from the particular stories and sayings which commonly circulated in the teaching of the writer's own church community, and that he had been commissioned to collect his community's traditions and to organize them in a way that seemed good to him. It is probable that the book was originally intended to be read aloud in the community's meetings for prayer and worship.

Little could the evangelist have imagined that his work would be so influential. In no time at all copies of it were circulating amongst the network of small Christian communities around the eastern Mediterranean, and his little book had become a foundation document for what was later to become one of the world's great religions.

THE GOSPEL TODAY

Over recent decades, Mark's Gospel has been the subject of the most intense scrutiny. In a large theological library, the scholarly books studying and analyzing its mere sixteen chapters can fill several shelves. This situation is in distinct contrast to the general disregard with which this Gospel has been treated in previous centuries. Then it had seemed an inadequate specimen of a Gospel, when compared to the lengthier Gospels of Matthew and Luke. But now that Mark's Gospel has been recognized as the earliest of all the written Gospels, it is treated as one of the first extended statements of Christian faith, and its author has come to be regarded as one of the earliest Christian theologians. In other words, although this Gospel primarily recounts the story of Jesus, it incidentally also conveys much information about the faith of Christians who lived in the generation after him. So in the commentary that follows, a good deal of attention is paid to this evidence.

But for all that this is a second-generation interpretation of Jesus, it also gives us much historical information. The Jesus who emerges is somewhat different from the idealized figure often presented by the Christian church. For the Jesus of Mark's Gospel is a strikingly Jewish figure, in a markedly Palestinian setting. In fact, modern Jewish scholars have begun to break the traditional silence of their race about Jesus, and have begun to use this Gospel as an important source of evidence about first-century Judaism. The commentary that follows frequently emphasizes the Jewishness of Jesus, and tries to speak in a way that is not exclusively Christian. Likewise, to avoid giving offence to non-Christians, dates are expressed according to the Common Era (CE/BCE instead of AD/BC).

Ironically, however, it has come to be increasingly recognized that the Gospel reflects the feelings of a Christian community who were trying to distance themselves from Judaism, and therefore comes across in places as anti-semitic. This fact seems to explain the evangelist's rather jaundiced view of the Pharisees; it also explains the pronounced way in which the blame for Jesus' execution is put on 'the Jews'. It is important that discussion of the Gospel text should acknowledge this tendency.

The notes which follow aim to avoid pious comments. They also refrain from speculating about what may have been going on in the mind of Jesus. They concentrate on explaining the evangelist's intentions and the impact that his text will probably have had on his first readers. This policy has been adopted in the conviction that Mark's Gospel is a fascinating book in its own right—as well as a foundation document for Christianity.

John the Baptist prepares the way

Along a road miraculously cut through a desert landscape comes a procession of people. They are bearded Semites in colourful woven clothes, just like those from the time of Abraham who were trading neighbours with the ancient Egyptians and who are recorded in Egyptian tomb paintings. The procession continues beneath, submissively submerged in the waters—this time taken from carved reliefs on a victory obelisk of Assyrian conquerors. The procession leads up to the towering figure of the Baptist.

The symbolism of this page hints at the long procession of Hebrew history which precedes the story that this Gospel has to tell: a recurring theme of captivity and release—first from slavery in Egypt, then from exile in Assyria and Babylon, and now (as this opening text implies) from a spiritual captivity. Indirectly, the page seems to invite readers to join in the procession as they follow the story which is about to be told.

The Gospel begins with a quotation from an ancient prophecy. When it was originally proclaimed to Jewish exiles in Babylon (about 540BCE), this prophecy gave hope of an early release and return to the Jewish homeland. But here it is seen as being further fulfilled by the historical figure of John the Baptist. The details of his style of food and clothing identify him beyond doubt as a prophet, like Elijah of old. That is astonishing, for prophets were considered to be an extinct breed. And what this prophet announces was intended to leave the reader in high anticipation.

For his sustenance John the Baptist relied on honey from the honey bee, *Apis mellifera*, locusts, *Locusta migratoria* (according to Leviticus 11:22, locusts were classified as acceptable food for Jews, although the eating of most other insects was banned), and the fruit of the carob tree, *Ceratonia siliqua*, whose beans provide a pulse food.

The wall painting is from the tomb of Khnumhotep at Beni Hasan, Egypt, which dates from about 1900BCE.

The large figure is from the relief of Sennacherib's capture of Lachish, now in the British Museum. It dates from about 700BCE.

The smaller figures are from Shalmanezer III's Black Obelisk, also in the British Museum and dating from about 850BCE.

Jesus is baptised

The viewpoint is that of Jesus at the moment of baptism—emerging from the water and looking upwards to a dove which is about to land gently. Behind it the sky is radiant. The far bank of the river is edged with dense vegetation which gives way to barren desert. Readers are invited by the very perspective of the illustration to identify with Jesus at this critical moment.

The Baptist's announcement has heightened our expectations: who is this person of whom he speaks? At that very point, Jesus appears on the scene. Nothing is said about his background, beyond the fact that he is from the village of Nazareth in the northern province of Galilee. He himself submits to the ritual of baptism, during which he has a religious experience involving a vision. The words of the heavenly voice draw together two famous scriptures. Psalm 2 formed part of the coronation ceremonies of ancient Judah's kings in which a father/son relationship was ritually established between deity and monarch. The 'Servant Song' from Isaiah envisaged Israel having a special role as bringer of justice to the nations of the world. What may we expect from a person granted such a vision?

The habitat of the rock dove, *Columba livia*, includes the inland cliffs and caves along the escarpments of the rift valley through which the River Jordan flows.

In its lower reaches, the river meanders through desert terrain, although along its banks grows a dense riverine forest of tamarisk, *Tamarix aphylla*, with Euphrates poplar, *Populus euphratica*, in its lower saline reaches and willow, *Salix alba*, further upstream.

This desert strip, within a day's walk of inhabited lands above the rift valley, has throughout history been a place of safe retreat for political refugees, guerrilla forces and religious recluses.

Jesus' temptation

A composite picture of wild and domestic animals and birds, all at peace with each other; beyond them stretches an empty rocky valley. The complexity and variety of the natural world displayed here is impressive. Some of the creatures are staring out of the page at us. They do not seem to be wary of us; rather, they are curious about the presence of a human being among them.

The waterpot, bread and branch of broom in the left inset are depicted against a desert background. They are a reminder of Elijah's perilous journey, in a previous age, through a similar desert to Mt Horeb.

Jesus' dramatic experience immediately leads to an extended period of retreat in the desert—traditionally the abode of hostile and evil forces. The last sentence tacitly implies that Jesus reclaimed these dangerous territories: he was able to live safely 'with the wild animals'. Humanity (at least this human being) and nature are at peace together, just like Adam in Eden.

Behind this story are two distinct ideas from scripture: first, a number of texts with a vision of an idyllic future state of earthly peace; second, stories of Israel's greatest prophets of old, Moses and Elijah, both of whom travelled to a desert mountain in order to encounter God.

In what follows, the Gospel story will frequently allude to Jesus' confrontations with evil forces resident within the human population; but here it is implied that he has routed these forces in their central stronghold. Frequent parallels will also be made between Jesus and the prophets of ancient Israel—especially Moses and Elijah.

Most of the species illustrated are still found in Israel: the eagle owl, *Bubo bubo*; raven, *Corvus corax*; kestrel, *Falco tinnunculus*; sheep (mouflon), *Ovis musimon*; wild ox, *Bos primigenius*; goat, *Capra hircus*; Nubian ibex, *Capra ibex*; cattle, *Bos taurus*; lion (now extinct in Israel), *Panthera leo*; leopard, *Panthera pardus*; Syrian bear (now extinct), *Ursus arctos*; wolf, *Canis lupus*; porcupine, *Hystrix indica*; viper, *Vipera palaestina*. White broom, *Retama raetam*.

Jesus' teaching about the kingdom of God

A luxuriant date palm flourishes on the fertile shore of the lake, typifying the plentiful abundance of Galilee after the barrenness of the Jordan Valley. This lofty tree seems to be in harmony with the page's message: it is at the stage when its fruit is about to be harvested—'its time has come'. Yet, until the moment of harvest actually comes, the fruit is tantalizingly out of reach, and its taste can only be anticipated.

Here is the first description of Jesus' teaching, encapsulated in three sentences, each making a special point. First, the time foretold in scripture when God would finally break into the world in judgment has arrived! Second, the longed-for rule of God overcoming the forces of evil is at hand! Third, people are invited to turn round ('repent') and look at the world in this light—for such news is good news ('gospel') indeed! So the first impression we are offered of Jesus' teaching is that it was about the nature of God and not primarily about himself or about ethics, as is often supposed. The phrase 'the gospel of God' emphasizes this point.

Much of the language has been chosen deliberately to have several levels of meaning. For instance, the word translated 'repent' basically means 'turn back'; this might involve turning away from a former way of life, with consequent repentance for sin. But it was also a word used in later Christian preaching, as is the word 'gospel'. So the phrase 'repent and believe the Gospel' is ambiguous: to the first readers it sounded like the challenge of a Christian leader's sermon ('repent of your sins, and believe the gospel—that in Christ you are forgiven'); but in Jesus' own message the sense was different ('turn back and believe the good news that God's rule is finally breaking in on the world'). There is yet a further ambiguity: 'Repent and believe the gospel' is a challenge to readers to take to themselves the truth of all that follows in this Gospel's narrative.

The Sea of Galilee is situated in a rift valley, 210 metres below sea level. This geographical depression results in a semi-tropical climate within the valley, such that the date palm, *Phoenix dactylifera*, is grown there commercially today. The inspiration for this picture is the view from the shore at Ein Gev.

The first disciples are called

A fishing boat, quite empty, is somewhat hazardously anchored and swinging in the wind. Its sail has been furled, although a net is still trailing from the ship and steering oars are still in the water. It shows all the signs of having been abandoned in rather a hurry.

The inset emphasizes the focus of many gospel stories—a fish. But in the context of this page's story, it is also worth remembering that, in early Christian art, the symbol for a Christian was a fish.

Every reader knew just how important Simon and the others later became: was it not the preaching of these very men that directly or indirectly was the source of the reader's faith? They had indeed become 'fishers of men', just as Jesus' word-play had jokingly prophesied.

And how resolutely these first four disciples respond to the call that day—just as Elisha had responded to the call of his future master, single-mindedly slaughtering his means of livelihood. It cannot have been easy for parents like Zebedee to appreciate.

Many of the gospel stories are about following Jesus, and the challenge to do so single-mindedly, whatever the cost. Now, right at the beginning of this Gospel, these first disciples are presented to readers as models who responded to Jesus decisively.

The Sea of Galilee is an inland sweet water lake supporting about twenty-five species of fish. The species illustrated is today called St Peter's fish, a *Tilapia* of the *Cichlidae* group. This carp-like fish makes very good eating.

The lake lacks any natural harbours, but recently a great deal of evidence has come to light about the maritime development around its shore in ancient times. The present surface level of the lake is about two metres higher than it was in the time of Jesus; but during periods of drought (most notably in 1986) its level drops, revealing the remains of ancient harbours and anchorages in at least thirteen sites. These remains consist of breakwaters, jetties and quaysides built with large field-stones and boulders. For example, at Magdala (the home of the Mary mentioned later on in the Gospel) there survives the remains of a breakwater sixty metres wide and seventy metres long, enclosing a harbour basin covering an area of one acre. This would provide safe anchorage for a very large number of vessels. In fact Josephus records that in 68CE he was able to requisition a fleet of 230 ships from the region of Magdala for a sea-battle against the Romans. This kind of evidence suggests that in the time of Jesus the Sea of Galilee was being exploited by a large-scale fishing industry. So it is probably quite incorrect to suppose that Simon, Andrew and the other disciples were uneducated peasant fishermen: Zebedee's business was large enough to have hired hands.

An evil spirit is expelled

The Jewish community of Capernaum have left a fine memorial in their synagogue, carved in stone and built on a grand scale. Although not a building that Jesus ever saw (it replaced the synagogue of his day), this is the building that present-day pilgrims to Capernaum see. It is a reminder of the Jewishness of Jesus, and the utter Jewishness of his teaching. Carved stone fragments from the building in the upper right margin emphasize the point: the magen or Star of David, and the menorah or lampstand.

We have heard a little of what Jesus taught. Now we are shown the effect of his teaching. Something about it amazed people: they felt he had an authority about him, and this authority made him quite different from their usual religious teachers. That authority seems to have been recognized not only by humans but also by spirits. One particular spirit recognized that, through Jesus, evil powers were about to be destroyed. And the exorcism proved the point: at Jesus' word of command, the spirit fled. The kingdom of God was indeed near.

It was taken for granted, in the first century, that evil spirits (termed 'demons') existed, and that they could inhabit ('possess') a human being, dementing them, and even speaking through the possessed person's mouth. Some people with healing powers were able to exorcise ('cast out') such spirits—as stories from surviving ancient literature outside the Bible bear witness.

The carved fragments from the ruined synagogue include a series of Jewish motifs. Clockwise from left they are a bunch of grapes, a Corinthian capital incorporating the temple candelabrum, the head of a creature (possibly a lion), a lintel with Ark of the Law, the *magen Dawid*, a *menorah*, the Ark on a wagon and a palm tree.

Healings

An artist's impression of a corner of Capernaum. It is Peter's house, imaginatively reconstructed on the basis of the actual foundations of walls uncovered by archaeologists. Several small houses are clustered in a random way around an open courtyard. An enclosure wall gives privacy from the lanes outside. The edge of the town gives way to cultivated land. The building seems to be home to a busy extended family, while the idyllic countryside bespeaks the story's healing peace.

The dramatic and very public exorcism in the previous story is followed, immediately, we are told, by a healing of a much more private, domestic and commonplace sickness. In no time at all, neighbours have gathered with their ailments and are healed. We are meant to understand these healings as further signs that the kingdom of God was near—for everyone believed that healing came from God.

This part of Capernaum was excavated in 1968, revealing that an elaborate octagonal church had been constructed in the fifth century directly over a collection of small domestic dwellings, which at different times had undergone a series of alterations and enlargements. At the lowest (earliest) level, dating from the first century, was a small rectangular room; scattered within its floor deposit were iron fish-hooks! This archaeological evidence suggests that during the period of the (Christian) Byzantine Empire, when pilgrimages to the Holy Land were an important part of Christian practice, an expensive shrine was constructed over the the house-church where Capernaum's Christians had met in earlier days before it was legally possible for them to construct church buildings. This house-church had at its centre what had originally been a private domestic dwelling—Peter's house. This interpretation is strengthened by the evidence of a Christian pilgrim called Egeria, who visited Capernaum in the latter part of the fourth century. She wrote: 'In Capernaum the house of the Prince of the Apostles (meaning Peter) became a church. The walls, however, of that house have remained unchanged to the present day'.

The illustration shows part of the town's quayside, and is based upon recent underwater discoveries (see the notes to page 17). There is a series of jetties, each projecting about thirty metres out into the lake from a stone quayside running eight hundred metres along the shoreline. Capernaum was a busy port, serving as a transit point for many passing through this region. So it was a strategic point for Jesus to have chosen as the base for his operations in Galilee.

Jesus praying and preaching

Two views of Galilee. Above, the landscape as Jesus may have seen it while standing on the stony shore of the lake in the calm of first light, before anyone has stirred. Below, a 'bird's eye' perspective of the hilly province of Galilee shows it touching the western (lower) shore of the lake, and criss-crossed by a network of roads linking the towns and villages of a thickly populated region. There is a puzzle about how to relate the near with the distant view, the immediate and local with the far-flung and regional, and this same problem is the one that confronts Jesus.

We have already been offered two glimpses of how Jesus' inner spiritual life was maintained—through a period of retreat (after his baptism), and through weekly formal corporate prayer in the synagogue on the sabbath. Now we are given a further glimpse. If it was intended over the previous two pages to give an impression of a typical day in the life of Jesus, then this page completes the daily routine by suggesting that it was his practice to rise for solitary prayer before dawn. This had been the practice of devout individuals since Old Testament times.

The aerial view (with the east at the top of the picture) gives a clear impression of the Sea (or Lake) of Galilee sunk in a deep bowl and surrounded by steep slopes on its east and west shores. The River Jordan flows into the lake at the north end, and out again at the southern end, and on southwards to the Dead Sea—the lowest spot on the earth's surface. The Jordan Valley depression forms part of the enormous rift in the earth's surface which runs from the Caspian Sea through the Red Sea and the East African rift valley system to the Mozambique Channel.

Jesus' ministry seems to have been chiefly confined to the province of Galilee, a relatively small region to the west of the lake. An impression of the small size of the area may be judged from the fact the it was easily possible to walk from Nazareth to Capernaum in a single day. Galilee was inhabited by people of Jewish race and religion, but surrounded on all sides by peoples of other religions.

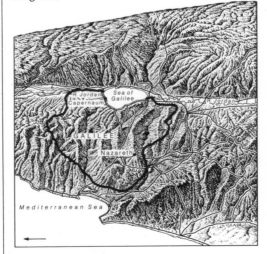

Leprosy healed

This page symbolically emphasizes the Jewish background to Jesus' activities. Mt Sinai (where Moses received the Law) towers above a desert plateau on which is pitched the Tent of Meeting. In front of it stands the altar, where the people's offerings were presented before the presence of the invisible God. Depicted above are the various offerings and materials required by the ancient ritual law for the formal ceremonial cleansing of leprosy. The page presents an impression of the ordered complexity of ancient rituals, all carefully observed in obedience to divine revelation on the holy mountain.

Leprosy was terrifying, not only because of its deforming effects on the body but also because of its social effect. To protect itself from infection, the community cast out sufferers, who would then have to fend for themselves. Moreover, sufferers were regarded as ritually 'unclean'. The chances of cure and restoration to the community were minimal: healing leprosy was reputed to be as difficult as raising the dead.

Knowing all this, the first readers of this story will be very surprised at Jesus' dramatic action in touching the man. They will be impressed by the strength of Jesus' emotional response to the outcast, and the simplicity of the healing (by a word and by touch). But the story is also making a 'political' point: Jesus is not encouraging disregard for the Law of Moses: it is possible to be clean and keep the Jewish law—a central conviction of the earliest Jewish Christians.

The reconstruction of the Tent of Meeting is based on the description in Exodus 26 and 27. The upper panel includes many of the items mentioned in Leviticus 14: a rock dove, *Columba livia*; a turtle dove, *Streptopelia turtur*; a cedar tree, *Cedrus libani*; a dye press and vat; hyssop, *Origanum syriacum*; a bowl for shaving and washing; oil and flour; a desert dweller's tent.

The word commonly translated 'leprosy' was used in ancient times to describe various skin diseases as well as true leprosy. The cures presumed by the Levitical rituals thus probably refer to this wider band of diseases.

Paralysis healed; a dispute over authority

The viewpoint is from inside the room where the healing recounted on this page took place. Above, the flimsy roof has been broken open. Below lies the woven mat on which the paralysed man had been lowered through the hole in the roof. It is empty, for he has been healed. The border is filled with fragments of broken plaster, apparently cascading down from the damaged ceiling.

The previous page and many later references tell of unmanageably large crowds and the strategies Jesus was compelled to adopt to cope with them. But here it is the resourceful strategy of four unnamed men which is emphasized: so great was people's belief in Jesus' healing powers that they would resort even to damaging property in order to touch him.

Paralysis is a strange disability. Although it can result from physical causes, it can also be brought on by fear and guilt. Is this why Jesus, rather than give a healing touch, in this case speaks a word about forgiveness? Whatever the reason, his word provokes a controversy, and he takes the opportunity to teach from it.

He builds his teaching around the authority of the obscure figure of the 'Son of Man'. This phrase (borrowed from a strange vision in the book of Daniel) is to be found only in the mouth of Jesus. It seems to have been a mysterious title which he chose to use when speaking of himself in a veiled way—particularly when he was challenging accepted religious traditions and claiming to do so with God's authority.

When the paralysed man actually got up and walked away, Jesus' claim seemed to all to be vindicated.

The plaster fragments are based upon some of the numerous pieces of plaster discovered by archaeologists during the excavation of Peter's house at Capernaum (see page 19). It was found that the roughly built walls had been plastered at least three times and decorated with designs including leaves, fruits and crosses. One hundred and thirty-one inscriptions, chiefly in Greek and Aramaic, had been scratched as graffiti on these plaster walls. Published in 1972, they include the names of Jesus and of Peter. The uppermost inscribed fragment in the border is a prayer in Greek which reads: 'O Lord Jesus Christ help . . . and . . . ' (the two personal names are now indecipherable).

Levi called; a dispute over sinners

A dish of grilled fish, which might have been served at Levi's feast. Above, silver coins from the period are a reminder of how despised he was because he collaborated with an oppressive government by collecting tax money.

This is a story about another controversy. Like many of the stories collected in this Gospel, it seems to have been preserved in the oral tradition of the first Christians for the sake of its final punch-line. It was very important to them that Jesus had been willing to associate with the poorer classes of society and had shared food with people who were regarded as despicable by Jewish religious leaders of his day.

The first readers of this Gospel were well aware that there had been running disputes amongst the first generation of Christians as to whether or not Gentile believers were obliged to keep Jewish ritual food laws. Without agreement on this matter, it was impossible for Jewish Christians and Gentile Christians to sit at the same table together. This story spoke to such divided Christians: Jesus himself shared food even with turncoat tax collectors, who could be regarded as no better than Gentiles since they earned a livelihood from the Gentile authorities employing them.

The Pharisees are presented in this Gospel as a religious movement within Judaism which was constantly in conflict with Jesus. Its members lived their daily lives in precise observation of Jewish ritual law, and they were themselves good living people, if puritanical. From their viewpoint, it seemed impossible for a religious man to count 'sinners' among his friends. By contrast, Jesus' life-style seemed to be proclaiming a quite different religious truth: despised tax collectors and 'sinners' were welcome in the kingdom of God.

■ *Tax collector* Capernaum was a transit port, where merchandise coming from the towns on the eastern shore was landed. Herod Antipas took the opportunity to extract a tax (or customs duty) on goods entering his territory here. Levi seems to have been one of the customs officials.

The fish illustrated is 'St Peter's Fish', grilled over charcoal.

The coin on the left is a silver stater of Augustus, Roman emperor at the time of Jesus' birth (he ruled from 27BCE to 14CE); in the centre are the reverse and obverse of a Tyrian tetradrachma, a common currency in the region between 126BCE and 65CE; on the right is a silver denarius of Tiberius, Roman emperor throughout Jesus' adult life (he ruled from 14 to 37CE).

Dispute over fasting

A newly made wine skin, recently filled, lies bulging upon a patched cloth. The tension between old and new material is clearly evident. The luxuriant vine above betokens the luscious fruit and flowing wine of a wedding feast.

Yet another controversy, this time about the religious custom of fasting. Jesus and his followers are criticized for not conforming to an austere self-discipline like some other Jewish sects. Jesus replies in a manner that is typical of him: not with reasoned argument, but with three analogies from everyday life—wedding feasts, repairing clothes and filling wineskins.

Readers familiar with the scriptures will have known that the analogy of marriage had been a favourite image of the ancient prophets in speaking of the relationship between God and Israel: God had chosen Israel as his bride, married her at the exodus, and called her apart into the wilderness on a honeymoon period of affectionate openness. Since that time the relationship had deteriorated and the wife had deserted her husband. But the prophets also hoped for a resumption of the joys of first love (as the quotations from the prophets Hosea and Isaiah indicate).

In hearing of the wedding feast analogy, Christian readers will also have caught Jesus' allusion: the time for the hoped-for resumption of first love has come, and, moreover, the bridegroom is here in the person of Jesus.

Such ideas burst out of the categories of contemporary Jewish thought, as the first readers were well aware: had not their Christian community torn away from traditional Judaism?

The vine, *Vitis vinifera*, was grown to supply both fresh and dried fruits. But the majority of the grapes were used for wine-making. The wine was stored either in large earthenware jars or in leather 'bottles' formed from the complete skins of sheep or goats.

A dispute over the sabbath

Central to the page are two ears of wheat and twelve loose grains, evocative of the dispute recounted here. Beneath them are twelve loaves of the 'bread of the Presence', as they might have been laid out for the temple ritual alluded to in Jesus' speech. The high-priestly vestments of breastplate and turban form the corner pieces.

A fourth story about a controversy with religious authorities, this time about observance of sabbath laws. Did picking ears of corn amount to reaping, and thus to breaking the ban on labouring on the sabbath day?

On this occasion, Jesus answered in the manner of the scholarly argument of the period: by identifying a passage of scripture which by analogy permitted or approved the case he was making. The passage he picked was of a famous incident when King David's men, on the run and desperate for food, had eaten the bread of the Presence, contrary to religious law. The implied conclusion is that in exceptional cases, the Law might rightly be regarded as subordinate to human need. In taking this attitude, Jesus was not at variance with rabbinic teaching, which included the saying: 'The sabbath is a gift to you, you are not given to the sabbath'.

But the very last punch-line is at variance with rabbinic teaching. It seems to be a Christian comment. The first readers will have seen in it justification of their own community's refusal to impose sabbath observance on Gentile Christians.

Of the two main varieties of wheat grown in Palestine, hard or durum wheat, *Triticum durum*, was more commonly ground for flour and used for bread. All ancient wheats were 'bearded'.

The table was fitted with rings and poles for carrying it about, because it was considered too sacred to be touched.

The high priest's breastplate is described in Exodus 28:15–30: it was set with twelve different precious stones, each engraved like a signet with the name of one of the twelve tribes of Israel.

The turban with its engraved plate of pure gold is described in Exodus 29:36–38.

The discrepancy over the name of Abiathar is inexplicable. The priest at the time of the incident referred to was Ahimelech, *father* of Abiathar. Faulty memory has come into play somewhere along the line.

A dispute over healing on the sabbath

Deserted streets surround an imposing synagogue. Within its walls, we may imagine the populace gathered to witness the confrontation described here. The apex of the gable starkly points to the equally stark conclusion to the story.

A fifth story showing how Jesus came into conflict with Pharisees. The issue is the same as that on the previous page: whether or not human need should override the claims of religious law, especially regarding sabbath observance. Once again, Jesus is presented to us as someone who invariably regarded human need as paramount, even above traditions considered to have divine origin in sacred scripture. He seems to respond with deep emotion to the human need planted in front of him, and with profound anger against structures of religion which leave adherents silent in the face of human suffering.

By now we are aware that the Gospel's compiler has deliberately collected together a series of five once-independent stories. Through them, we are being invited to notice, right at the beginning of the account of Jesus' life, what were the causes which brought about his end. It is being suggested that these conflicts are typical of the grounds on which several authorities, including the religious (represented here by Pharisees) and the secular (represented here by Herodians), would eventually combine to destroy Jesus.

The illustration shows a reconstruction of the synagogue at Capernaum as seen from the same perspective as the ruins on page 18. The synagogue's white limestone (imported from outside the region) contrasts sharply with the local black basalt of the domestic buildings. In the shadow of this great synagogue, Capernaum's early Jewish-Christian community met to pray in Peter's small house (see page 19). The contrasting style of buildings speaks something of the rivalry between the two communities of faith. In the early decades, the minority Jewish-Christian community felt oppressed. This may account for the rather poor light in which Pharisees and other Jewish leaders are presented here and elsewhere in Mark's text.

The reconstruction of the synagogue is after that by Watzinger (1916).

Crowds follow Jesus

A boat is moored by the quayside, its sail ready hoisted. It is Jesus' get-away boat. Out of sight, a crowd is pressing its incessant demands; but ahead the lake is calmly inviting, and beyond it the quiet hills offer a refuge.

This paragraph deliberately contrasts with what we have been hearing. If there was opposition from religious authorities, we are being encouraged to recognize that there was also widespread support from the common people. In fact, it is implied that people flocked to Jesus from every part of the land inhabited by the Jews (see the map below).

If they were attracted by self-interest in his healing powers, we, the readers, know a little more about what was going on: these healings were signs that the kingdom of God was drawing near in the person of Jesus.

Here we meet the title 'Son of God' for the first time in the narrative. It is a scriptural title, originally applied to King David and his successors on the Jerusalem throne (who were never thought of as anything but human). But by now it is clear that the narrative is inviting us to treat this title in some further supernatural sense.

In 1986, the hull of an ancient ship was recovered by archaeologists from the mud of the lake's bed near Kibbutz Ginnosar. It is constructed from cedar wood planking and oak frames, scientific tests proving that the timber was felled within the period 120BCE to 40CE. It is 8.2 metres long and 2.3 metres wide, was apparently crewed by four oarsmen and a helmsman, and was capable of carrying up to ten passengers as well. This is the first material evidence of the size and quality of boats from the Sea of Galilee in the time of Jesus; Jesus and the Twelve could certainly have sailed together in a fishing boat of this type.

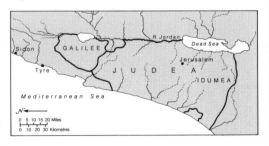

The Twelve appointed

We are looking back over the winding track along which we have walked up from the lake shore near Capernaum. At this height, the distant view is panoramic, and even today our eyes can see very much the same view that Jesus and his disciples once saw.

This apparently simple paragraph is packed with symbolic meaning. The key to its interpretation is in the number twelve—which immediately suggests an allusion to scriptural ideas surrounding the twelve tribes of ancient Israel. Just as that twelve-fold body was formed into the covenant people of God at Mt Sinai, so here (it is implied) Jesus is forming the 'new Israel' around himself on another mountainside. In fact, listening carefully to the sequence of the last two pages, we notice that after the confrontation in the synagogue Jesus 'withdrew with his disciples', and now he is appointing twelve leaders of a new community. It feels as though the later separation of synagogue and church has already begun.

The function of the Twelve is to preach and drive out demons—that is, to share with Jesus the task of bringing in the kingdom of God. We are thus led to expect an intensification of the encounter with the powers of darkness.

The view is that seen from the road to Safat, at a point where the entire circumference of the lake is in view. In the time of Jesus, the north and west shores (from Capernaum westwards) were densely populated and the surrounding land intensively farmed. Because of the geological depression, the climate at the shoreline is tropical, while a few kilometres away on high ground the climate is more temperate. Josephus, who had lived in the area in 67CE, describes the wide variety of fruits cultivated: 'There is not a plant which this fertile soil refuses to produce, and its cultivators in fact grow every species . . . The walnut, a tree which delights in the most wintery climate, here grows luxuriantly beside palm-trees, which thrive in heat, and olives and figs which require a milder climate. One might say that nature had taken pride in thus assembling . . . the most discordant species in a single spot' (*Jewish War*, 3.10.8).

A dispute over Satan

The main door into the house is ajar; a neighbouring door is fast shut, while a third door has been left open into a courtyard. The illustration invites a double interpretation: it is the house where Jesus is teaching, and crowds have gained entry by every means possible; but it is also the house alluded to in Jesus' teaching which has been burgled. In the border, representations of three ancient pagan Canaanite deities hang menacingly over the house, symbolic of the destructive or binding powers of evil.

We have just been led to expect a confrontation with the powers of evil—and on this page it comes. It comes through what seems to be a perverted perception, twice over. First, Jesus' most intimate circle, his immediate family, attempt to silence him, thinking he has gone 'out of his mind'; and second, a distant circle (although one extremely influential in forming public opinion) announced the twisted conclusion that Jesus was demon-possessed himself.

The text has been cleverly written, with one story told inside the other, so that one illuminates the other. Far from Jesus appearing out of his mind, he is shown mustering an acute argument to counter the charge of being possessed by a demon called Beelzeboul. As ever, he speaks pictorially: a strong man's house cannot be successfully burgled unless the owner is first rendered powerless. By implication, this imagery suggests, Jesus could only be working the healings and exorcisms (which we have already been hearing about) if God himself had first bound the powers of evil—a secret which we, the readers, were let into on page 18. Now healings were generally regarded as the work of God. So to suggest that they were the work of a demon must have seemed such a perversion of truth that it could only be described as 'blasphemy'—that is, defiant hostility to God. Someone holding such a view must be perceiving good as evil, and so could not be forgiven, for they were denying the very God who could forgive them. Some such logic seems to lie behind the notion of 'an eternal sin'.

The house is a reconstruction of Peter's house, but the viewpoint is different from the one on page 19.

The three objects in the border are based upon Canaanite artifacts discovered by archaeologists. At the top of the page is a stone stele carved in bas-relief, depicting Baal, the thunder and rain god; the embossed gold sheet in the centre is a fertility amulet depicting Astarte, goddess of love and Baal's consort; below is a bronze figurine of Baal carrying shield and spear. Baal continued to be worshipped in the time of Jesus among the non-Jewish population of neighbouring Semitic peoples. The name Beelzeboul seems to include within itself the name of the Canaanite deity.

The parable of the sower

The flat open country and grain fields are viewed from such a low angle that what is most noticeable is a trodden path winding its way into the field. It is stony; huge thistles partially block the view; seed-eating birds are everywhere; the depth of soil in the field on the left looks very shallow. At all points, there seem to be impediments to the harvest.

At long last, we are offered in this chapter some detailed examples of what Jesus actually taught and of his style of teaching through parables. To judge from this example, a parable is a story or observation about everyday life, told in such a way as to leave the listener pondering. But the parable itself does not directly say what it means: it is a kind of riddle, told to provoke the listener to reflect and, it is to be hoped, to find enlightenment. Yet the final sentence on this page implies that Jesus does not expect everyone to get to this point.

We ourselves are left puzzled by the parable of the sower. Its meaning is not immediately obvious. The emphasis of the story is plainly upon the fantastic yield of the crop in the end, despite various hazards along the way. But, without knowing the context of discussion within which Jesus first told this parable, we cannot be sure of its original meaning. We only have the story itself, preserved as a memorable utterance from his mouth.

Nevertheless, by placing the parable in this position, after so many stories of rising opposition and conflict, the evangelist seems to be suggesting reason for hope. It is the same reason that the sower has for hope—the fact that the seed which he sows contains life within itself.

The milk thistle, *Silybum marianum*, may well be the 'thorns' of the parable. This plant, common around cultivated land, has a natural habit of producing a rosette of large leaves, flattened to the ground; thus it ensures space for itself by smothering any smaller or slower-growing plants.

The house sparrow, *Passer domesticus*, is very common around any human habitation. Like the rock dove, *Colomba livia*, flying higher up, it frequents cornfields in search of grain at sowing and harvest times.

Interpretation of the parables

It is as though the viewer is standing amongst a line of reapers, stooping down to the corn and looking up at the next row to be cut. The array of grain still waiting to be harvested is impressive for its sheer abundance.

The first paragraph is very puzzling. Can Jesus really have taught in parables with the deliberate intention of making his teaching obscure to those 'outside'? It seems improbable. Where, then, did the evangelist get this idea from? The best explanation seems to be that this parable (and many others too) had been passed down in oral Christian tradition, but without any reference to its original context. So its precise meaning was in fact obscure to later Christians. They therefore presumed that this obscurity was intentional, and jumped to a further conclusion: that this explained why the Jews failed to respond to Jesus during his lifetime. The failure of Jews to welcome the Christian message was the greatest intellectual problem confronting early Christians, and they comforted themselves with the knowledge that a famous prophet like Isaiah had been no more successful in convincing earlier Jews of his God-given message. So the pattern of Jewish rejection of God's message, evident in ancient scriptures and in Jesus' own life, seemed to them to have been divinely ordained.

The second paragraph likewise seems to spring out of an early Christian setting: it appears to be a Christian sermon, using Jesus' parable of the sower as its text. The parable is treated as an allegory, so that each feature in it is taken to correspond to an aspect of the Christian community's experience. The sower is a Christian preacher; the seed corresponds to 'the word' (Christian jargon for 'the gospel'); the mixed response to the preaching reflects the Church's experience—in particular, 'persecution . . . because of the word' undoubtedly refers to later Christian sufferings. The effect of the sermon is to challenge the congregation to consider which kind of soil they are.

The grain illustrated is emmer wheat, *Triticum dicoccum*, the second of the two ancient wheats grown in the region (compare page 25). Emmer, still grown today, is one of the ancestors of our modern wheats. Each seed produces a main shoot, caller a tiller, and several secondary tillers. Depending on the fertility of the land and the year's weather, the plant may produce several fertile ears, one on each tiller. Since each ear can have between twenty and thirty grains, it is actually possible, in exceptional circumstances, for a single grain to produce a hundred-fold yield. But for a whole field to do so was beyond a farmer's wildest dream.

More about parables

Images from two of the parables frame the page, emphasizing the mystery of growth, the fascination of flame and the joy of harvesting.

The first two paragraphs are constructed out of once-independent sayings of Jesus, whose original context (and precise meaning) had been forgotten. Some of the sayings sound like traditional proverbs. But now they have become linked together in such a way as to continue the theme of perceiving spiritual truth.

On this interpretation, the light of Jesus' teaching may be hidden for a while—but it has been revealed privately to the disciples, who will in due course publish it openly. The spiritual meaning of Jesus' teaching becomes apparent only to those who already possess spiritual insight—the parables increase their insight, while anyone without insight is left even more bewildered by the parables.

The context in which Jesus told the parable of the seed growing is also lost. But in its present position in the Gospel, we seem to be meant to apply it to Jesus' own teaching activity: once sown, his teaching was bound to lead to a harvest. The parable was also an encouragement to dispirited Christian preachers: their task is simply to sow the seed and not to worry about immediate results, for it is God who will bring about the harvest—not human will or effort.

The illustration on the left shows the development of a main stem (tiller) of wheat. The ear is just emerging from the last leaf (the flag). Later, it will extend above the flag to swell and ripen in the sun.

In the picture on the right the sickle surrounds what could be a single plant, with one main and two secondary tillers, thus indicating a possible yield from one single seed (see the note on the previous page).

The pottery lamp burnt olive oil for fuel. Such lamps were mass produced in moulds and were common objects in every household of Jesus' time.

The parable of the mustard seed

An imaginary landscape, with a prominent mustard plant in the foreground, explores the symbolism of Jesus' enigmatic saying by contrasting the weak stem of the mustard plant with the majestic cedar tree in the distance.

Another parable about growth from small beginnings. Early Christian readers may have reflected on the parable in the light of similar ideas in the visions of Ezekiel and Daniel. In that case they may have treated the parable as an allegory—with the birds in the parable corresponding to Gentile converts, who after Jesus' lifetime had found 'shade' through the preaching of the Christian gospel. Gentile Christians will have been fascinated to discover that their presence in the church was anticipated in this piece of Jesus' teaching, which (as we have already seen) is generally very Jewish in character.

This parable, and the others in this chapter, hold before us the ultimate success of Jesus' activity, at a point in the story when we have been made powerfully aware of the forces of opposition ranged against Jesus (see pages 26 and 29).

To round off this section of Jesus' teaching, it is emphasized once again that the disciples required constant private explanations.

Black mustard, *Brassica nigra*, was common in the region. It has conspicuous clear yellow flowers. The flowers in turn produce pods which contain the many very small seeds, a delight for seed-eating birds. The plant, being an annual, grows fast up to a height of about two metres.

The cedar, *Cedrus libani*, from the mountain forests of Lebanon, was greatly prized for its timber.

Jesus rebukes a storm

A nightmare scene: the bow of the boat is pitching violently into the waves; the rope securing the mast has snapped; behind, the sail and rigging must have collapsed; the vessel is filling up fast with water; at any moment it may be overwhelmed.

This dramatic story can be read at several levels simultaneously. Evidence of an original event involving a near sinking seems to be provided by two particular nautical details (see below), which are preserved like fossils within the text; neither would be likely to be mentioned in a purely imaginary story told for theological effect.

Nevertheless, the language used to tell the story shows all the signs of much reflection upon scripture. In particular, the extraordinary use of the verb 'rebuke' suggests a direct parallel with Psalm 104 and implies that the wind is thought of as a personal force. Likewise, the command given to the waves ('Be still') literally means 'Be muzzled' and is the very same word used by Jesus to the evil spirit on page 18 (there translated 'Be quiet!'). All this implies that the first tellers of this story considered the storm to be the work of personal demonic forces out to destroy Jesus. There was good precedent for this idea, since the Psalms often used the image of waves and engulfing deep waters to depict the forces of chaos opposed to God. In this light, we are intended to see the story as akin to the earlier stories of exorcisms and healings—in each case the control of evil powers is seen to be broken by Jesus. Wherever he is present, it is apparent to us readers that 'the kingdom of God is near' (see page 16). Yet despite the witness of their eyes, the disciples do not seem to grasp this momentous fact.

The Sea of Galilee, being situated in a deep bowl-like depression, is liable to sudden squalls: any fast air currents moving over the surrounding plateaus become turbulent as they pass over the depression.

Two small details within the Greek text may reflect what is now known about the construction of Galilee fishing boats. Jesus is said to have been sleeping 'in the stern' and 'on the pillow'. The craft discovered at Ginnosar (see page 105c) appears to have been steered by a helmsman who stood on a small half-deck at the stern of the ship. The space beneath this little deck would have been the most sheltered spot on board, the only place where anyone was likely to be able to sleep. The Greek words that are translated as 'a cushion' should more accurately be translated as 'the pillow', and the implication is that it was a normal part of the boat's equipment—most probably a sandbag, commonly used as ballast for such ships.

A demon-possessed man is healed

Two manacles, blood-stained from chafing on the wrist, hang empty. Their captive is free and he has left behind him the sharp stones with which he wounded himself in his demented state. Beneath lies a desolate valley with shaft tombs in which he once lived and a rough track leading up the hillside to where the pigs are foraging. The imagery speaks of release from a terrible torment.

This story builds upon the astonished question with which the previous page ended. There Jesus had successfully overpowered a storm demon; here he is confronted by an entire army ('legion') of demons, who had taken up residence in an unfortunate man.

The original readers will have been aware of a number of symbolic allusions in the story. First, the whole event is happening outside Jewish territory, amongst the Gerasenes, a people whom the Jews would regard as 'pagans' and 'Gentiles'; so the story is about the power of Jesus to deliver people imprisoned by fear of the many gods of paganism. Second, the fact that the man lived 'among the tombs' implies that he is symbolically living in the realms of death; the story shows that Jesus is able to rescue him even though he is at the extreme edge of human society—so the story is about a resurrection from death to life. Third, the drowning of the huge herd of pigs can be taken as a sign of the extinction of these Gentile demons; so the story is about how the kingdom of God was dawning even in Gentile culture, through the presence of Jesus. The earliest Gentile readers will have been delighted to recognize in the story insights that they themselves had gained through coming into the Christian faith.

■ *region of the Gerasenes* See the note on the next page.
■ *lived in the tombs* It was common for bodies to be buried in shafts cut horizontally into rock faces. Disused tombs were thus like caves in which a person could find shelter.
■ *pigs* An ancient law (Deuteronomy 14:8) forbade Jews to eat pork, probably because the sacrifice of pigs was an important ritual for pagan Canaanites. As a result no Jewish farmer would consider keeping the animals. By contrast, Greeks relished pork. The presence of these animals is a typical sign of Gentile culture. The species illustrated is *Sus scrofa* and is native to the Near East.

Gentile Decapolis hears of Jesus

An aerial view looking down upon the territory of Decapolis—the 'Ten Cities' which were independent city-states, proudly founded three centuries earlier to promote Greek culture. For a brief moment, the focus of the story is on non-Jewish people, and the illustration emphasizes how Jesus was not unwilling to step into such territory, even though it was 'pagan'.

To the first readers, the fascination of this story was that it showed that Christian witness to the Gentiles began within Jesus' own life-time, and was in fact inaugurated by Jesus himself. The healed man became a missionary to his own people, in effect fulfilling the words of Psalm 105.

■ *the Decapolis* A Greek name meaning 'Ten Cities' and referring to territory settled by the Greek soldiers from Alexander the Great's conquering armies. Each city was an independent democracy, but together they formed a loose federation of rich commercial centres along the trade route from the Red Sea to Damascus. Parts of the city of Gerasa (Jerash, in the modern Kingdom of Jordan) were excavated between 1925 and 1956, revealing a very extensive city with an elaborate grid system of colonnaded streets, a theatre, a forum, and a temple dedicated to Zeus in 22CE.
■ *region of the Gerasenes* The reference on the previous page poses an historical problem. Gerasa (called Galasa by Pliny) is about sixty-four kilometres/forty miles south-east of the lake and never held territory reaching to its shore. The parallel story in Matthew's Gospel speaks of 'the region of the Gadarenes'—that is, the people of Gadara. But that city also lies many kilometres from the lake. It seems that the name of the region got confused at a very early stage when this story was being passed on by word of mouth, and it is not now possible to identify where the events took place. In the fifth century, a Christian monastery commemorating the miracle was founded in a village called Kursi, on the eastern shore of the lake; it has been excavated and can be visited by tourists today. But the monastery's existence explains no more than a later Christian obsession with identifying gospel sites.

Pliny was a Roman historian and scientist with an encyclopaedic knowledge, whose *Natural History* summarized all that was known about the world and its peoples. He died while observing Vesuvius erupt in 79CE.

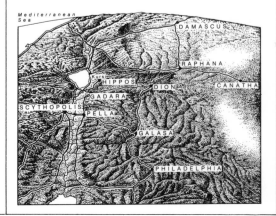

A woman is healed

A torn and worn-out rag, dropped on the ground, symbolizes the healed woman's release from the poverty to which her ailment had reduced her. No longer does she need to staunch her internal bleeding, nor vainly seek relief from a disorder which has made her both a social and a religious outcast.

Back once again on Jewish territory, Jesus' healing powers are publicly acknowledged by a leader of a local synagogue: this seems to be a new development, for up to this point synagogues have been places of opposition.

The Jairus story, however, is interrupted by another self-contained story, and will be picked up again on the next page. The interruption not only helps to indicate the passage of time but also gives us an important hint on how to interpret the Jairus story: the two narratives are told in such a way that they are both stories about particular incidents, yet also about every Christian's path to salvation.

Several phrases in the story of the woman's healing are deliberately ambiguous and open to two meanings simultaneously. She had heard 'the things concerning Jesus' (a peculiar phrase, which to a Christian reader could also mean the contents of Christian preaching about Jesus). Then she had sufficient trust in what she had heard that she was moved to act. Finally, Jesus commended her with words that have two meanings at once: 'Your faith has healed you' can equally well be translated 'Your faith has saved you'. Thus the story about this particular woman is also an illustration of Christian teaching about how a person may come to salvation through Jesus.

It is hardly a coincidence that this story and the two previous stories are about people who, humanly speaking, were at the end of their resources: the woman had spent all she had; iron chains could not bind the demonic power; the boat was being swamped. Yet the presence of Jesus saved each of them in their extremity. With these three stories in mind, we wait in anticipation, wondering what may happen to Jairus' daughter, hovering on the extremity between life and death.

The story about the woman is a self-contained unit, which may once have circulated on its own in Christian circles. Its construction shares many features in common with other Jewish and Greek miracle-stories: a description of the ailment, the failure of previous physicians, the healing and its public confirmation.

A dead girl is restored to life

The scene is viewed through a half-opened door. Light floods in from behind the viewer to a room that had been in darkness—the darkness of death. A water jug, bowl and beaker ready to give drink to the parched throat or to wash the body remain beside the death-bed. But the bed itself is empty. Apparently the girl has got up and walked out into the light only just a moment ago.

After the interruption of the story of the woman's healing, the Jairus story is picked up again. But in the meantime, his daughter has died. Taking a clue from the intervening story, we may expect this story to have a double meaning too. And so it had for the first readers, for it seems to illustrate Christian teaching about death. Thus, the bereaved father is told not to be afraid but to 'believe', for the child is not dead but only 'asleep'. This idea brings scorning laughter. These aspects of the story echo Christian perceptions of death. Because of their belief in the resurrection of the dead, early Christians described their dead as 'sleeping', since they believed that they would one day be awakened into eternal life. For this belief, they were laughed at by pagans; nevertheless, early Christians buried their dead with joyful singing and even held fellowship meals over their graves.

So it seems that this is the fourth of a group of stories in which Jesus confronts and overcomes the worst powers of darkness, including even death itself. At the very least, Jesus is shown to be not inferior to the great prophets Elijah and Elisha, each of whom restored a dead child to life.

■ *Talitha koum* These two Aramaic words are deliberately preserved in the Gospel's Greek text. They sounded as strange to the first readers as they do today in English. The reason for preserving them seems to have been a desire to record the very sound of Jesus' words, which had such power that they restored the dead to life. It is not impossible that early Christian healers may have wanted to utter the same words themselves. *Talitha* literally means 'lamb'. In English, 'little lambkin' would capture something of the affectionate tone of endearment which the word suggests. *Koum*, however, is grammatically incorrect because it is the masculine gender; it seems that the proper word (*koumi*) became shortened as the story was transmitted by word of mouth among Christians who were ignorant of Aramaic.
■ *not dead but asleep* Paul habitually preferred to speak of Christians falling asleep rather than dying (see 1 Corinthians 11:30 and 15:6, and 1 Thessalonians 4:13–15 and 5:10).

In his home town—a prophet without honour

A corner of the carpenter's workshop. Two completed jobs lie propped against the wall: a threshing sledge set with sharp flints, and a window frame. A half-made ox-yoke leans against the bench. They are reminders of a village's expectations of its carpenter, in making and repairing agricultural implements and items for domestic buildings. With what incredulous tones of voice did former neighbours exclaim, 'Isn't this the carpenter?'

We have already had hints that some people were sceptical about Jesus. Now we are shown that those with whom he had grown up in his home village are frankly incredulous. He has returned like a rabbi 'accompanied by his disciples', and is giving formal teaching in the synagogue. Although they acknowledge the wisdom of his teaching, they cannot square it with their intimate knowledge of his humble artisan origins.

In fact, the uncomplimentary way in which they call him 'Mary's son' seems to hint at some suspicion about his legitimacy, since Jewish men were always identified by reference to their father.

All of this gives Jesus the chance to quote a well-worn proverb about prophets being honoured everywhere except at home. The earliest readers will have appreciated the implication that Jesus was a 'prophet', for in their eyes he was indeed the prophet that Moses had spoken of. Moreover, the story on the previous page has just shown how Jesus' activities were like those of the great prophets Elijah and Elisha.

■ *carpenter* The Greek word *tekton*, here translated 'carpenter', can refer to a craftsman working in wood, stone or metal. So building, blacksmith's work and carpentry may all have been a part of Jesus' trade. In about 160ce, a Christian teacher from Palestine wrote: 'When he was on earth, he used to work as a carpenter, making ploughs and yokes' (Justin Martyr, *Dialogue with Trypho*, chapter 88). Thus a century after his lifetime, Palestinian Christians considered Jesus to have been a village craftsman manufacturing agricultural implements with both metal and wooden parts.
■ *the brother of James* There is evidence from elsewhere that later on 'James the Lord's brother' became leader of the Jewish-Christian community in Jerusalem. He presided at the Council of Jerusalem (Acts 15:13), and a little later Paul made a deliberate point of meeting him during a brief visit to Jerusalem (Galatians 1:19).

The tools on the bench include a sharpening stone, bow-drill, chisel, mallet, adze, saw, dividers and hammer. A bow-saw leans against the bench. A large adze and plane stand beside the threshing sledge.

The Twelve sent out on a preaching tour

It seems that two of the Twelve, who are on their travels, have been offered hospitality here. They have just gone inside the house and have left their walking staffs and sandals by the doorway. Will they need to shake the dust off their feet here tomorrow?

We first heard of the Twelve in chapter 3 (page 28), when they were appointed so that they 'might be with him and that he might send them out to preach and to have authority to drive out demons'. In the meantime, they have listened to his teaching (chapter 4) and witnessed his mighty works (chapter 5). Now at last they are sent out on the task for which they were appointed. The theme of repentance in their preaching seems to resemble Jesus' own initial proclamation, and they too exorcize demons and heal the sick—just as Jesus had done (on pages 18 and 19).

Very specific travelling instructions are given, from which we get the impression of an intensive teaching campaign around the villages of Galilee. Distances between villages were small, and people would have known each other. It was reasonable to expect to be offered hospitality for short periods of time. So the Twelve are to travel light: carrying nothing with them except a traveller's staff, wearing only light sandals, not even bringing a change of underclothes (tunic).

Reading between the lines, the purpose of the campaign seems to have been to prepare the people of that region for the coming of God's kingdom. There was an urgency, and a warning as well. If a village was unwelcoming, the messengers of the kingdom were to perform a symbolic action which all could see. They were to shake the dust of that unresponsive village off their feet as they left. Jewish villagers would know well what that sign meant: that their village was being regarded as heathen territory (see below). It was a warning which might make them think again.

■ *shake the dust off your feet* Strict Jews performed the same symbolic action whenever they re-entered Palestine after journeying abroad. The idea was to avoid contaminating God's holy land with the dust of profane places. Villagers who saw the disciples do this would recognize that their village was being marked, to all intents and purposes, as heathen—and liable to the fate reserved for the heathen when God's kingdom came.

The sandals are based upon first-century sandals found by archaeologists at Masada in the Judean desert. The thick leather soles (without heels) were fastened to the foot and ankle with leather thongs.

King Herod's fear of Jesus

The desert fortress of Machaerus, built as a refuge by King Herod the Great to ensure his own safety from subjects who hated him. The palace residence at the centre of the fortifications seems to offer fantastic views over the rocky landscape—a dream residence for an excessively wealthy and paranoid ruler.

Several stories over the last few pages have left us wondering how to classify Jesus in our minds. For example, some of his healings have seemed to rival those of Elijah and Elisha, and he apparently regarded himself as 'a prophet' (page 39). Now, for the first time, Jesus is explicitly associated by name with Elijah—at least in the opinion of some. This encourages us to believe that we were indeed correct in supposing that the evangelist expected us to make mental comparisons between his stories of Jesus and the ancient stories of Elijah.

However, another popular opinion was that Jesus was John the Baptist returned from the dead. Since this is the first mention of John's death, the evangelist naturally proceeds to tell us how he came to meet his end—at Herod's hands. It is an elaborate story, and continues on the next page.

■ *King Herod* Herod Antipas, son of Herod the Great. He ruled Galilee and Perea from 4BCE to 36CE. In about 17CE, he founded Tiberias as a Roman city from which he ruled Galilee. There is historical uncertainty about the relationship of 'King Herod', Herodias and Philip. According to the Jewish historian Josephus (writing about 94CE), Herodias had been previously married not to Philip, but to another half brother of Herod Antipas, also called Herod; Josephus also says that Philip married Herodias' daughter. (The problem of the historicity of the gospel account is discussed further in the notes to the next page.)

The text does not state where John was imprisoned. But we learn from Josephus that John was imprisoned and executed at Machaerus, a great fortress perched on the top of an isolated mountain east of the Dead Sea, in the territory of Perea.

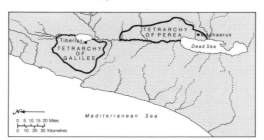

John the Baptist is beheaded

Inside the fortress, the scene is set for Herod's birthday celebrations. There are musical instruments to accompany entertainments of song and dance, and an extravagant banquet is spread out. In the centre, an empty golden platter awaits its grisly load.

The story begun on the previous page continues here. It is the only story in the Gospel which can be compared with an independent account of the same events preserved elsewhere. If we compare this text with the extract from the Jewish historian Josephus (placed in the margin of the previous page), we quickly notice that the two accounts do not entirely tally—not least because the guiding interests of the two writers differ. Josephus is concerned primarily with political questions, but the Gospel deals with theological questions.

The comparison helps us to perceive the reason why this lengthy story is included within the Gospel at all. At first sight, the story feels like an intrusion, basically unrelated to the Jesus story—for in fact it differs from all the other stories of the Gospel by not having Jesus as its chief actor.

The account of John's moral stand and the gory details of his execution, however, do reflect on Jesus. They show that John was a true prophet (when everyone thought prophets were an extinct breed), and that John suffered and died for his prophetic stand. A little later in the Gospel (page 57) it will be revealed that Jesus considered John to have been 'Elijah'.

Now if Elijah has indeed returned (in the person of John), then 'the great and dreadful day of the Lord' can be expected to follow quickly. That conclusion will easily be drawn by every Christian familiar with Malachi's prophecy (placed in the margin of the previous page). All of this implies that Jesus is to be the agent for bringing in the 'day of the Lord'. It also implies the likelihood that if Jesus continues to act prophetically, he too will come to a similar end at the hands of the state authorities.

Three kinds of musical instruments are included: wind, string and percussion. From the left they are the lyre, a rattle, clappers, a harp, cymbals, a tambourine, a flute, a trumpet, pan-pipes, a double trumpet and a *shofar* (ram's horn).

The banquet has a Gentile flavour about it: the jug and goblets are of Roman design and some of the dishes, such as lobster and the suckling pig, are non-kosher (that is, food unacceptable to Jews). Other delights include roast beef served with olives and onions, roast chicken, bread, stuffed vine leaves, grapes, olives, pomegranates, figs and dates.

Jesus seeks solitude with his disciples

Evening light from a low setting sun still touches distant mountains. Twilight is approaching. Echoing the page's story, sheep are scattered around, for the broken down sheep-pen is much in need of repair.

We last heard of the apostles ('the Twelve') as they set out on a preaching tour. Now they return and are offered a period of quiet refreshment alone with Jesus. But their intention is thwarted by the ever-insistent crowd. We are reminded of Jesus' own desire for solitude, and how it was thwarted in similar fashion (page 20). So the disciples are slowly coming to know their master's own experience.

Early Christian leaders will have sensed a parallel with their own experience of pastoral work and will have been challenged by Jesus' attitude to 'sheep without a shepherd'.

However, the chief purpose of these two short paragraphs is to prepare the setting for the great miracle that is to follow, among a large crowd in a remote place.

Five thousand people are fed

Baskets everywhere. Twelve of them. They are empty and ready to be used to collect the left-over fragments from a mere five loaves and two fish. It leaves the mind baffled, and searching for the story's meaning.

The earliest readers of this astonishing story will immediately have made three connections. First, they will have known the story of how the Israelites were miraculously fed by God in the desert on their way to the promised land. Second, they will have noticed that Jesus' fourfold action exactly corresponds with what he did later at the Last Supper (page 85). Third, they will have been aware that the ritual actions at their own worship gatherings included the same four actions of taking bread, giving thanks for it, breaking it and sharing it.

Jesus' actions correspond with those of any Jewish host entertaining guests at a feast. But clearly this whole occasion is also highly symbolic. Moses fed the Israelites in the wilderness on the way to their Promised Land; and Jesus feeds his followers, also in a deserted place, as they prepare for the coming kingdom of God. So this desert feast is a kind of anticipation of the 'heavenly banquet' which Jews expected at the end of time.

Early Christian readers will have interpreted this story as yet another sign that the kingdom of God was dawning.

■ *eight months of a man's wages* (a very loose paraphrase of the Greek words 'two hundred denarii') A *denarius* was a Roman silver coin. According to one of Jesus' parables (in Matthew 20:9), a manual worker would be paid a 'denarius' for a day's wage. Two hundred denarii thus amounted to about eight months' wages— not the kind of sum the disciples would be carrying about with them.

■ *taking the five loaves* The traditional Jewish ritual for beginning a meal when guests were present was for the host to take bread, to pronounce the 'blessing' over it, to break it, to give portions to the guests, and to start the meal by eating a portion of it. The 'blessing' was a prayer thanking God for the food, such as: 'Blessed are you, O Lord our God, King of the universe, who brings forth bread from the earth'. The story on this page follows the same pattern.

Present-day tourists to Galilee are shown the Church of the Multiplication of the Loaves and Fishes at Tabgha. This cannot be the authentic site, since it is right beside the road to Capernaum and by no means the 'remote place' required by the text. However, a very famous mosaic design of loaves and fishes is preserved in the floor of this ancient church.

The disciples cross the lake in safety

A very low perspective focuses attention on the anchor-stone lying beneath the clear water. This still water contrasts dramatically with the tempestuous waters through which the disciples had desperately rowed in the earlier part of this page's story.

Another extraordinary story, which offends the modern rational mind. A clue to its meaning for the evangelist seems to be contained in his curious judgmental remark about the disciples: 'they had not understood about the loaves'. What should they have understood? What is the connection between the feeding and the lake-crossing? Apparently, the previous page's story should have clarified the meaning of this page's story; but the disciples, although they are so close to Jesus, have missed the point of both.

The evangelist wanted to stress this, because it helped his readers answer their critics. To the criticism, 'If Jesus really was the Son of God, why was it not obvious to people at the time?', the answer is offered, 'Because their hearts were hardened (by God)'.

However, with hindsight, Christian readers could see the complementary symbolism in both stories: the desert-feeding anticipated entry to the Promised Land, and the safe lake-crossing actually brought them to the land— just as Joshua had led the Israelites dry-shod across the waters of Jordan.

Early Christians may also have applied this story in another way. Embattled by persecution, they may indeed have known that 'the wind was against them'; and they may have drawn encouragement from believing that the Lord saw them 'straining at the oars', and that he himself (no phantom, but the Living One, Master of winds and waves) would surely come quickly for their salvation, even though it be in 'the fourth watch of the night'.

The drawing of the anchor-stone is based upon examples of such stones found on the lake bed at many of the anchorages around the shore (see page 102b).

The word of God and the traditions of men

Water is being poured from the lip of a pitcher for hand-washing. It seems cool and refreshing. How did this become a cause of religious contention?

The first readers will have followed the arguments on this page and the next with close interest, for they seemed to speak directly to an issue which had split the Christian community: how far were Gentile Christians obliged to observe Jewish ritual regulations? This was not a hypothetical question, for it affected community life in basic ways. For instance, some Jewish Christians were unwilling to share a meal with Gentile Christians if they had not ritually cleansed themselves and their cooking vessels and household crockery. Was there any evidence as to what Jesus thought about the matter?

The interest of this passage is that it seems to suggest that Jesus took the liberal rather than the strict view. He quotes back to the Pharisees a case (perhaps an actual case that had recently happened) which was obviously contrary to natural justice: a man had refused to support his parents in old age on the grounds that he had, with an oath, given away his money to the temple. It was a hard case to judge, because scripture contained not only a law about honouring parents, but also a law about not breaking an oath. Apparently some Jewish lawyers had given precedence to the oath rather than to the parents' needs. Jesus, by contrast, gave precedence to human need.

■ *These people honour me with their lips* The quotation is from the Greek version of Isaiah and differs from the Hebrew text in the last two lines.

■ *Corban* An Aramaic word meaning 'an offering'. It had the sense of gift devoted to God, which was thus placed under a religious taboo, and could not be used for any other purpose.

Clean and unclean

A page with symbolic images about Jewish dietary regulations. Above, a cheese and a joint of lamb—each of which (in a religiously observant Jewish home) would have to be prepared in separate kitchens within the same household. Beneath, a pottery vessel lies smashed on the floor, perhaps because it was discovered to be 'unclean'. The flour that was in it is wasted on the ground, but someone has drawn in it with their finger, to illustrate a point from the last paragraph.

Scripture contains elaborate dietary laws defining 'clean' and 'unclean' food. In particular, the last sentence in the left margin ('Do not cook a young goat in its mother's milk') became the basis for subsequent orthodox Jewish regulations designed to ensure that dairy products and meat products could not contaminate each other, by having them cooked and served in separate kitchens. The laws in the right column require an astonishing scrupulousness on the part of any Jewish housewife. Any food eaten in defiance of these laws was considered to make a Jewish person 'unclean'. That is why Jewish Christians were so uneasy about eating with Gentile Christians (see the previous page, and also below).

For the first readers, the fascination of Jesus' teaching on this page was that it offered a totally different concept of uncleanness. Without actually counter-manding the scriptural laws, Jesus insists that it is what comes out of a person (not what enters them) that defiles a person. From this teaching, one very early reader (with evident delight) deduced the conclusion: 'In saying this, Jesus declared all foods "clean"'. These words are now placed in brackets, because they do not seem to be from the evangelist himself; they appear to be a marginal jotting by a later reader, which then got copied into all subsequent manuscripts. The jotting itself is fascinating, for it is evidence of the kinds of way the earliest readers used the gospel text— searching it for teaching which might resolve contentious issues in their own church situation.

Evidence of disputes amongst the earliest Christian communities about dietary laws is to be found in the letters of Paul (Romans 14:14–15 and 1 Corinthians 10:23–32), and in the decisions of the Council of Jerusalem (Acts 15:19–20); also in Peter's difficulty in acting consistently (Acts 10:10–15 and Galatians 2:11–13).

A Greek woman's faith

A couple of dogs are licking up scraps under a table. Another is sitting up, looking us straight in the eye, begging for a choice favour just as the woman in this page's story also begged a favour.

Tyre and Sidon were two trading ports whose territory bordered on northern Galilee. In ancient times they had been enemies of Israel (as the quotations from Ezekiel suggest). Basically Gentile in culture, they were a good place for Jesus to seek peace and quiet from Galilean crowds. Yet even in Gentile territory his reputation as a healer cannot be hidden, and a Greek (presumably pagan) woman seeks his help. What follows is like many other healing stories, although their recorded exchange suggests that Jesus enjoyed witty repartee, and accepted it from a woman.

The chief interest of this story, however, lies not so much in the healing it reports as in the location of the event in Gentile territory. In fact, according to the arrangement of the Gospel's material, from now on, until chapter 10, when he begins the journey south to Jerusalem for the final confrontation, Jesus spends most of his time outside Galilee.

This seems to be a piece of deliberate editorial policy. The evangelist has already prepared us over the last two pages by showing us Jesus' liberal interpretation of Judaism's most exclusive teachings. Now we are shown Jesus active outside the Jewish heartlands. Early Gentile Christian readers will have seized on this story as justification of the church's decision to extend its preaching and membership to Gentiles.

Jews regarded dogs as abhorrent and despicable scavengers; they were not welcome as domestic animals in a Jewish household. Greeks, by contrast, often kept pet dogs. This being so, Jesus' conversation with the Greek woman is remarkably apt: he seems to be enjoying a cross-cultural dialogue.

The dogs depicted on this page are Saluki hounds, an ancient Arab breed of dog found throughout eastern Mediterranean lands.

Another healing in Gentile territory

Not the usual map of Palestine. The land is seen from above Phoenician Tyre and Sidon (bottom left), looking southwards. The River Jordan seems to form a sharp divide between Jewish heartlands on its right bank and Gentile Decapolis on its left bank. Jesus apparently felt free to travel on both banks, and had no inhibitions about associating with Gentiles.

Another healing in the Gentile territory of the Decapolis. The account is unusual in several respects: very precise details of Jesus' healing actions are given—he takes the man aside, put his fingers in his ears, spits, touches his tongue, looks up, sighs, and utters the word 'Ephphatha'. The healing consisted in the fact that the man 'began to speak plainly', whereas previously he 'could hardly talk'. We shall simply note these details here, and discuss their significance later when we compare this story with that on page 53.

The account ends with these Gentile people being 'overwhelmed with amazement'; they 'kept talking about' what had happened. The Greek verb could equally well be translated 'kept on preaching' what had happened, for it is the very same word habitually used in Christian circles for preaching the gospel. Greek-speaking readers will have enjoyed the play on words and will have understood the symbolism of the story: the handicapped man corresponds to all the pagan world (unable to hear God or address him plainly); but once healed, there was so much to preach. Such a proclamation to such a people may have felt like 'streams in the desert' (Isaiah 35:6).

■ *Ephphatha* The Aramaic for 'Open!' Compare this preservation of the very sound from Jesus' lips with other healing words on page 38.

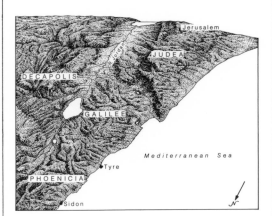

Four thousand people are fed

Seven flat loaves of bread and a couple of handfuls of small fish. Together they wouldn't even fill a single one of the fishermen's baskets. Haven't we heard a story like this before? Why are we being told it again?

This story is so similar to the one on page 44 that most of the comments made on that page apply here also. The similarities include the remote location, the question 'how many loaves do you have?', the command to sit, the words over the loaves, the statement 'the people ate and were satisfied', the fragments gathered into baskets, the dismissal of the crowd and a journey in a boat. The only substantial differences are over the number of people, the number of loaves and the number of baskets.

Even more surprising is the fact that the events following this story seem to mirror the series of events following the feeding of the five thousand: by deliberate editorial construction, this part of the Gospel seems to be made up of two parallel series of stories—a feeding (pages 44 and 50); a lake-crossing (pages 45 and 50); a controversy with Pharisees (pages 46 and 51); a story about bread (pages 48 and 52); and a healing (pages 49 and 53).

What is going on here? What is the evangelist intending by such an organization of his material? Part of his purpose is to depict the dullness of the disciples, who cannot even see the meaning of things the second time round. This will be discussed more fully on page 114a.

But another part of his purpose may have been to offer us a symbolic contrast: the first feeding symbolizing the giving of the Bread of Life to the Jews and the second symbolizing the giving of the Bread of Life to the Gentiles. The second feeding seems to have happened on Gentile soil (in the Decapolis), and it thus enacts the words of Jesus to the Greek woman, when he insisted that 'the children' (the Jews) should be fed first, and only then might 'the dogs' (the Gentiles) have some crumbs (page 48). In which case, this is yet another story justifying the inclusion of Gentiles within the church's membership.

■ *baskets* The Greek word used here (*spuris*) describes a kind of basket made out of woven matting (as illustrated). It is known to have been a common fisherman's style of basket. A completely different word (*kophinos*), implying a wickerwork basket, is used on page 44; this is known to have been a specifically Jewish style of basket—a fact which fits with the symbolic interpretation of the two feeding stories. The fish illustrated are St Peter's fish and the lake sardine, *Acanthobrama terre sanctae*.

Seeking a sign from heaven

Overhead a striking cloud formation gives a passing hint that heaven might open and reveal its secrets. But a second look confirms that there is no 'sign' there. Down below, the rolling landscape passively continues in its mundane familiar way.

In asking for 'a sign from heaven', the Pharisees perhaps hoped for something like the signs given to Ahab or Hezekiah. To their minds, Jesus' teaching was sufficiently revolutionary to require a sign from God ('from heaven') if they were to accept it.

But in view of all the healings and feedings already recounted, it seems perverse to ask for something further—as perverse as the Israelites of Moses' day who 'tested' God in the wilderness, even though he had miraculously fed them there (Psalm 95). The irony is that Jesus has twice already performed the classic 'sign from heaven' of providing bread in the desert.

To the first Christian readers, these Pharisees must have seemed as blind as the people of their own day who failed to respond to Christian preaching. Why was it that they remained outside Christian faith, unconvinced by the Christians' teaching about Jesus? Why was it that some people could see signs, and others looking at exactly the same thing could see nothing of special significance?

These questions have already been raised on page 31, and they will be picked up again in the next few pages.

The blindness of the disciples

On board a fishing boat, sailing past a village on the shore-line. The provision basket is empty, and a single loaf on the bench is the only sustenance available.

The Pharisees have just shown themselves to be singularly blind. Using metaphorical language, Jesus now warns his disciples to beware of 'the yeast of the Pharisees'. But in their confusion, they completely miss the hidden point of his remark.

In what follows, Jesus wrestles with their incomprehension, and by patiently bringing the right questions to their notice, he begins the process of opening their eyes to see the meaning of all they have witnessed.

In telling this story, the evangelist is inviting the reader to identify with the disciples. In this story—and the next two as well—he is exploring the process by which every Christian comes to faith, insight and understanding. In the disciples' case, that process is to be a slow and gradual one, and (as the next two stories make plain) can only happen as a divine gift.

■ *yeast* Being a natural agent of fermentation, yeast was seen as a symbol of inner corruption. For this reason it was banned from temple offerings (see the left margin).

A blind man is healed by stages

A view from the track just outside Bethsaida, looking back at the village. In the field on the left, a gnarled old olive tree can clearly be seen. But up above is a nightmare scene of phantom-like trees. The illustration seems to suggest that first stages of growing in faith and insight may be as confusing as the blind man's partially restored sight.

This strange story holds an important place in the construction of the Gospel: it marks the conclusion of the series of stories following the second feeding (page 50), and has similarities with the healing story on page 49, which concluded the series following the first feeding (page 44). But more significantly, it marks the end of Jesus' public ministry in Galilee.

So the story stands at a kind of bridge point in the Gospel. From this point onwards, things will focus around Jesus' continuing attempts to teach his disciples in private and to open their eyes to see who he is. So this healing story has to be read on two levels. At the most obvious surface level, it is about an individual man from Bethsaida; but at a symbolic level, it is about all the disciples (especially Peter), who are slowly, by stages, coming to see clearly.

■ *village* It is quite incorrect to describe Bethsaida as a village. In the time of Jesus, it was a city in the territory of Philip (Herod Antipas' brother). Archaeological excavations conducted on the site (Et-Tell) from 1987 show it to have been of considerable size and wealth. This geographical inaccuracy seems to provide important evidence about the identity of the evangelist: he cannot have been an eye-witness, nor was he a native of Palestine, nor in direct touch with Peter, who was a native of Bethsaida.

Jesus predicts his suffering

The text of the Gospel seems to be written directly upon the beam of a light wooden cross. The design would seem to invite reflection on how far the Christian gospel actually is the story of the cross.

This page marks the first stage of the removal of the disciples' blindness. They begin to see who Jesus is, but not yet clearly. (We were prepared for this gradual process of illumination by the symbolic interpretation of the previous story (page 53)). Slowly and patiently Jesus prompts their insight through questioning; slowly, and inaccurately at first, they begin to see.

We ourselves have already noticed how earlier stories in the Gospel have implied that Jesus was seen to be acting like the prophets of old. But now a completely new title is used: 'the Christ'. Apart from the opening sentence of the Gospel it is the first time this now-familiar title has been used, so it is important to understand its meaning. It is a title—not a personal name—and in the Greek language means 'anointed one' (in fact it could perfectly well be translated with those two words here). It translates the Hebrew word *messiah*, meaning the same thing. Early Christian readers were accustomed to attaching the title to Jesus' personal name and undoubtedly believed that Peter was the first to do so. For them, the title sprang out of the scriptures, for in ancient Israel three kinds of people were anointed so that they could enter sacred office: priests, kings, and prophets—as the bottom left quotations show.

Jesus, however, does not seem to like the title. He orders them not to speak about it and avoids the title on his own lips. The word had political overtones (as an early title of kings), implying the use of force to bring in the kingdom of God. Instead, he prefers another title: 'Son of Man'. This is the first time Jesus has spoken openly about himself, and he uses the occasion to emphasize that he is destined to suffer and be killed—something that is quite beyond Peter's comprehension. Peter is still very far from seeing clearly.

But, as all Christian readers will have surely known, the story did in fact turn out exactly as Jesus here describes it. So this saying feels like a prophecy, which is to be fulfilled at the end of the Gospel's story. Once again, Jesus is behaving like the prophet foretold by Moses (see right margin).

■ *Caesarea Philippi* The capital city of the province ruled by Philip, Herod Antipas' brother. It lay at the foot of the massive Hermon mountain range, in the extreme north of Palestine, and outside strictly Jewish territory.

Jesus' followers must expect to suffer

On this page Jesus' disciples are warned that they must be ready to take up their cross and follow. Two visual images emphasize the starkness of the language. Above is the horizontal cross-beam which all condemned criminals had to carry for themselves on the way to execution. Below is a drawing of heel bones actually found in a Jerusalem tomb, transfixed by a massive nail.

For the first Christians, 'taking up their cross' was not a picturesque turn of phrase for 'bearing difficulties'. Every reader of the time will have seen crosses outside Roman cities. This hideous form of execution was reserved for violent criminals, slaves and traitors, and was designed to prolong their death agonies. The Roman philosopher Seneca even considered that the ignominy of suicide would always be preferable to crucifixion.

So the teaching on this page is a warning to the disciples (and the readers) that following Jesus may put their life at risk. The long quotation from Isaiah 53 was highly influential in forming Christian thinking about Jesus' sufferings.

In 1968, building development in Giv'at ha-Mivtar, a suburb of modern Jerusalem, revealed three caves used as burial places in the first century CE. They contained the bones of thirty-five individuals neatly placed in stone boxes (or ossuaries), with the names of the deceased scratched on the outside. In one box were the bones of a male aged between twenty-four and twenty-eight and those of a child aged between three and four. The two calcanei (heel-bones) of the man were transfixed with a single iron nail about eighteen centimetres long. It had been hammered first through a piece of wood, then through the right heel, the left heel, and another piece of wood; finally the point of the nail had been turned over to make it fast. It seems that the victim's heels had been nailed into a kind of frame, before he was fixed on the cross; the frame itself would then have been nailed to the cross. It is not impossible that he was crucified upside-down, with his weight hanging from his knees over the cross-bar, and his feet (in their frame) attached to the cross-pole on the opposite side to his body. It seems that when they came to bury him, his relatives were unable to extract the nail (because its point had been burred over), and they were compelled to lay out the corpse with the heels still nailed together, with the fragment of the frame still attached. On the outside of the ossuary two names were roughly scratched: *Yohanan* and (according to one reading of the crude writing) *Yohanan son of the one hanged with his knees apart*. Yohanan's bones are the only surviving remains from antiquity known to be evidence of a crucifixion. But they bear witness to a human capacity for cruelty which almost defies imagination.

Jesus is transfigured

Very high up in a mountain range, on the snow line, high winds are blowing snow and cloud across the scene, so that the summit is temporarily hidden from view. Why is the story set in this wild, if majestic, terrain?

The disciples have just been hearing some unpalatable teaching about suffering. But it seems the period of suffering may be relatively brief, for some present will not have died before they 'see the kingdom of God come with power'—a phrase suggesting God's reversal of the present world order at the end of time. This truly astonishing remark is immediately given sharper meaning in the story which follows.

'Six days' is such a curiously precise period of time that we are meant to notice it. It seems to imply that Jesus' prophecy of the first paragraph is in some sense fulfilled in the presence of three named disciples in the story of the 'transfiguration'. That word itself is a peculiar one, indicating that Jesus' physical form was changed, or transformed. Before the disciples' eyes his earthly form was transfigured so that they saw him in a glorified or heavenly form, in the company of two great prophets long dead—the very two about whom the Gospel has already shown great interest. How is such a vision to be interpreted? The answer is supplied by words from a cloud, which everyone would take to be the very voice of God: this is God's son, whose teaching (even the unpalatable bits) is to be heeded. Then immediately the vision vanishes, and they are in the presence of the Jesus they know.

In the succeeding story, will these disciples now be able to see any more clearly, or is their 'healing' still only partial? However it may unfold, the evangelist certainly intends the readers to read the second half of the Gospel in a new way, now that they have been given this glimpse into the hidden identity of Jesus.

■ *a high mountain* The precise location is not named. Since Caesarea Philippi (the city mentioned two pages ago) is adjacent to Mt Hermon, which is 2,814 metres high and snow-capped for much of the year, it is often assumed to be the mountain in question. However, for the first readers identifying the mountain was irrelevant; what was significant was that the revelation took place on a mountain-top, just like the famous revelation to Moses on Mt Sinai, recounted in Exodus 24 and 34.

More teaching about the Son of Man

On the way down the mountain, after a most incredible experience. Back at the edge of the snow line again, the first trees begin to appear—and beyond them the lower foothills and habitable lowlands around the distant lake. Down there, life will have continued as usual, oblivious of the mountain-top experience.

Three disciples have just been given a glimpse into the hidden identity of Jesus. Now, immediately afterwards, they are instructed to be silent about this revelation until after 'the Son of Man had risen from the dead'. This is such an obscure phrase, that it is not surprising that they were puzzled. In part, it picks up the the saying about the Son of Man on page 54. Jesus, however, does nothing to solve the disciples' puzzlement.

By contrast, the first readers—who already knew the end of the gospel story before they got there—could see that the transfiguration story was a kind of resurrection appearance, before the event: an anticipation of the resurrection itself. Naturally, it could not be spoken of before the resurrection had actually happened. So, once again, the readers of the story have an advantage over the disciples within the story—an irony which the evangelist seems to enjoy.

Readers have also already been informed about John the Baptist and his gruesome death (page 42, for example). They could therefore unpack the code language of the last paragraph: Elijah has indeed come (just as prophesied by Malachi) in the person of John the Baptist; but although God's prophet, he was not given divine protection. Instead he suffered and was killed. In the same way, the Son of Man cannot expect divine protection.

So this obscure saying is preparing the disciples (and the readers) to realize that, in descending the mountain, Jesus is choosing a destiny which is bound to lead to suffering—despite all that has been glimpsed through the transfiguration.

■ *the teachers of the law say . . .* It is possible that the sayings on this page helped early Christians to counter arguments of Jewish teachers. Certainly, one generation later, Christians were still encountering this kind of reasoning: 'We Jews all expect that Christ will be a man of merely human origin, and that Elijah will come to anoint him. If this man (Jesus) appears to be the Christ, he must be considered to be a man of solely human birth; yet from the fact that Elijah has not yet come, I must declare that this man is not the Christ' (Justin Martyr, *Dialogue with Trypho*, 49).

A spirit is cast out of a boy taken for dead

Fire and water—two terrifying elements which have threatened the life of the demented lad in this page's story. They appear as he may have seen them, when helplessly falling into flames or into deep water. How terrifying not to have control of our own body's actions; and how agonizing to see our own son in this state.

This is the last exorcism to be recounted in the Gospel. It seems to be yet another story about the disciples' inadequate faith—for the irony of the story seems to be that the boy's father possessed a faith in Jesus which was lacking in the disciples. Through the dialogue with the father, we are shown the process by which faith grows. At first the father appeals to pity, uncertain of Jesus' powers ('if you can do anything . . . '); Jesus questions the 'if', stressing that there is no limit to what God will do for people with faith; in his desperate need, the father bursts out in a declaration of belief—while in the same breath acknowledging its inadequacy. But that is sufficient.

But there is more to the story than an object lesson in faith. For the healing is described in words that are deliberately open to double meanings. The Greek text states that people said the lad was dead, but that Jesus 'lifted up' the boy and 'he arose'. The obvious meaning is that Jesus took the inert body by the hand, pulled the lad to his feet, and he stood up, as the NIV paraphrase indicates.

But there is also a second symbolic meaning to the story, for the two Greek words translated 'lifted up' and 'arose' are precisely the verbs used by early Christians for God 'raising' Jesus from the dead, or for Jesus 'rising' from the dead. This gives us a clue as to a second hidden second meaning of the story: it is a resurrection story. This is its message: if we are Christians and have faith, then even after our loved ones have become corpses and 'most people' consider them dead, the God who raised Jesus can, and will, raise them to eternal life. This hidden second meaning makes the story follow on very naturally from the transfiguration story: it seemed to be an anticipation of Jesus' own resurrection, and now this next story adds that through (the risen) Jesus, God will raise up the dead to eternal life.

The parallel with Moses continues. In some sense Moses was transfigured as a result of being on the mountain with God (his face continued to shine—see page 56); he too descended the mountain to find his deputies engaged in controversy and the people unfaithful; he too upbraided the people (Exodus 32).

A second prediction of Jesus' suffering

For a second time, the gospel text is written on the cross. Its grain is clearer now, more knotted. The perspective seems ambiguous. Is the cross obscuring the tranquility of the Galilee scene? Or is the tranquility displaying the cross?

We seem to have heard most of this before—which we have (on page 54). Once again, Jesus is teaching his disciples privately about the inevitability of his coming suffering. When he first disclosed this, he was in the extreme north of the country (at Caesarea Philippi); but now he is passing through Galilee—a good deal nearer Jerusalem. So awareness of his steady journey southwards dramatically heightens the sense of impending doom.

Once again, Christian readers, knowing full well how the story would end, had an advantage over the uncomprehending disciples. The evangelist almost seems to be using this dramatic device as though he would like his readers to break off and discuss amongst themselves why the disciples were so obtusely blind to the meaning of Jesus' plain words. Any such discussion would lead to a strengthening of the readers' own convictions about Jesus.

The new information given in this prediction is that Jesus is going to be 'delivered' (not 'betrayed', as the NIV incorrectly translates the Greek word) into the hands of his executioners. This unexpected word suggests a passive acceptance, without struggle by force to escape being handed over. All of this was quite contrary to common expectations of the Christ.

■ *Son of Man* Once again this technical term is found on the lips of Jesus, apparently as a hidden way of speaking of himself. But precisely what is implied by the title is left unclear. However, readers with a knowledge of the scriptures would know that 'Son of man' was a poetic turn of phrase used in Ezekiel's prophecy. In Ezekiel 2:1 God says: 'Son of man, stand on your feet and I will speak to you'. The phrase thus refers to Ezekiel himself, and simply means 'man'. Taken in this sense, Jesus' saying would mean: 'Man is going to be betrayed into the hands of men'.

Who is the greatest?

Twelve cups of water: six on one side and six on the other side of the pitcher from which they have just been filled. The pitcher itself seems to be symbolic of the servant-leader and his teaching.

We can begin to see a pattern in the construction of the Gospel here. After Jesus' first prediction of his suffering, Peter failed to understand, and the disciples were given teaching about taking up their cross (page 55). So now, after a second prediction of his suffering, the pattern is repeated: the disciples again fail to understand, argue about power, and have to be given teaching about being 'servant of all'.

As an accomplished educator, Jesus gives his teaching through an enacted visual aid: he takes in his arms a child, a powerless person without status, whose interests are nevertheless to be embraced. This is the kind of servant-leadership expected of his followers by one who is prepared to be 'delivered' into the hands of his executioners.

The whole subject of leadership was highly relevant to the first readers. The Christian community was still in the process of being established, and differing styles of leadership were being experimented with. Respect for the needs of 'little ones' (that is, poor people with simple faith) are held up here as important qualities in the Christian leader.

The clue that this page is really about styles of leadership in the Christian community is provided by the very last sentence. The phrase 'because you belong to Christ' sounds extraordinary in the mouth of Jesus (nowhere else in the Gospels does 'Christ' appear without the definite article). But the phrase was perfectly natural among the first generation of Christians (Paul uses it in Romans 8:9). So it seems that this saying of Jesus includes commentary by early Christian teachers.

■ *in my name* This phrase comes three times on this page and seems to be a kind of link between the three pieces of teaching, which otherwise lack any logical connection. Both here, and on the next page, link phrases are used several times to join up otherwise unrelated sayings of Jesus. This seems to be a sign that at an extremely early stage, long before the Gospel was written, collections of Jesus' sayings were organized for teaching purposes: the shared link phrases were a jog to the memory, reminding one which saying came next.

■ *Do not stop him* Jesus' refusal to act protectively of his own status bears a general resemblance to Moses' refusal to be jealous of other prophets in Numbers 11.

Causing little ones to stumble

An ingenious but simple mechanism for grinding corn in large quantities. The millstones seem to be of great size and weight: did they correspond to the gravity of the offence which brought them to Jesus' mind?

The teaching about pastoral care of the Christian community continues with a saying of Jesus, warning about the seriousness of causing 'little ones' to stumble in their faith. It is typical of Jesus' style to use exaggerated language to emphasize a point. A donkey-driven millstone had a central hole in it big enough to put a man's head through. But its sheer weight was far more than would be necessary to drown a person. The absurdity of using such a vast weight is meant to make us laugh and remember the point.

'Cause to sin' is an inadequate paraphrase of a carefully chosen Greek word which has the much more vivid meaning 'cause to stumble'. In which case Jesus' saying is about stumbling while travelling on the journey of discipleship and not at all about particular sins. Through the use of the link phrase 'cause to stumble', the teaching then flicks to causes of one's own stumbling. Again the language is exaggerated, and certainly not meant to be taken literally. Basically it is teaching about the need for self-sacrifice to enter the kingdom of God.

As for the last three sentences, their meaning is quite unclear. They are sayings of Jesus once upon a time spoken in a specific setting about a particular situation. But their context is now lost, with the result that nobody can now be sure what the sayings mean. The sayings themselves, however, were preserved by the Christian community because they were known to be sayings of Jesus, and therefore precious.

The technique noted on the previous page of linking unrelated sayings by common link phrases continues here. There are at least five once-separate sayings, now linked together (probably for easier memorization) by the phrases 'cause . . . to stumble', 'fire' and 'salt'.
■ *millstone* The Greek word specifically refers to a donkey-driven stone, like that illustrated (and not the small grindstones turned by hand by a housewife).
■ *hell* A misleading paraphrase of the NIV. The Greek text has the word 'Gehenna', which should not be translated. Gehenna was the name of the deep valley to the west of Jerusalem where the city's refuse was dumped and burned in a seemingly unending fire. Consequently, the name became proverbial as a place of filth and fire, a picture of the imagined torment of the wicked after death. Thus it seems that the later Christian doctrine of 'hell' and eternal punishment were not in Jesus' mind at all; once again he is using exaggerated language in making a point about the serious possibility of stumbling and falling out of faith.

Jesus teaches the dignity of women and children

A page with writing materials. At the top is a papyrus document, folded and sealed; below are a wooden pen-case, quill pens and a hanging bronze ink-pot. With these instruments, a document could be written legally dissolving a marriage.

The geographical note at the beginning of the chapter is important. According to the scheme of this Gospel, all Jesus' early ministry took place further north, in Galilee. This north country is the territory of revelation. But now, Jesus finally leaves it and enters the province of Judea, in which Jerusalem was situated. Judea and Jerusalem in particular are to be the territory of confrontation and the final climax of the gospel story. Throughout this chapter there is a sense of impending conflict, as Jesus moves steadily closer to Jerusalem.

No sooner is he in Judea than he is challenged—on his interpretation of religious law. The issue chosen by the Pharisees was whether it was lawful for a man to divorce his wife. The question was a curious one, because everyone knew that the Law of Moses (Deuteronomy 24) certainly did permit a man to do this in specified circumstances. Jesus, however, does an extraordinary thing: he rejects this law as a 'second best' compared to God's ideal intention for marriage. He justifies his attitude by quoting from the first book of the Law (Genesis). This was clever: he could not easily be accused of disregarding the divine law.

While Jesus' stance on divorce may at one level sound 'hard line', at another level it acted to protect the position of women, who were disadvantaged in Jewish culture through the Mosaic Law.

The next incident concerns another disadvantaged group: young children. This time it is his own disciples whom he confronts—yet another example of their failure to see clearly.

■ *if she divorces her husband* This saying makes no sense in a Jewish context, where it was not legally possible for a wife to initiate divorce proceedings. The situation envisaged can only have happened in a Gentile setting. For example, in Roman law either party could initiate divorce. So the amplified teaching given in private 'in the house' sounds like a later development of Jesus' teaching to meet the situation of Christians living in Gentile settings outside Palestine.

The pen-case, ink-pot and papyrus document are drawn from actual examples surviving from the Roman period. The case was found in Egypt, with remains of black ink in its well; the ink-pot was recovered from the River Tiber; the document was found in a cave near the Dead Sea.

A rich man fails to follow

A picture that might have flashed across the mind of Jesus' questioner at the moment his face fell. Laid out on a rich purple cloth are precious items from his wealthy household: vessels and jewellery, and semi-precious stones still waiting to be cut or mounted. Behind are lengths of uncut cloth; above, a beautiful and intricate ornament. The page speaks not only of property acquired, but also of hopes and intentions. The uncut and unmounted stones in particular symbolize the future plans he might have had to forgo if he was to follow Jesus.

This story is deliberately placed here as yet another example of how Jesus' attitude challenged accepted Jewish attitudes. It was commonly believed that wealth and possessions were a sign of God's favour; although alongside this, it was also taught that the rich had a responsibility to give alms to the needy. It came therefore as a great surprise to this man to be told that he should dispose of his entire source of income—the means by which he could do righteous works.

Nevertheless, once again the story makes plain that Jesus did not despise (nor fundamentally contradict) the scriptures. On the contrary, he seems to respond warmly to the fact that the man had been brought up since childhood to keep the revealed Mosaic Law. In fact, this man is the only person in this Gospel of whom it is said that 'Jesus . . . loved him'.

The reason for Jesus' warm response seems to be connected with the man's opening question: he earnestly desired to 'inherit eternal life', a Jewish phrase meaning to 'enter the kingdom of God'. He seems, therefore, to have been thirsty for the very thing Jesus had been announcing.

The story's message, however, is that the man was living with a false assumption: that he had to do something to earn eternal life, whereas the one thing needful was to follow Jesus. Later on, Christians were to teach that eternal life is a free gift from God, which cannot be earned by anyone, however virtuous (as in Ephesians 2:8–9). So the first Christian readers will have sensed that this story very sharply illustrated the central meaning of the Christian gospel—and, moreover, that there is a cost to following Jesus.

Items depicted are based upon objects surviving from the Roman period: a gold cup, a silver jug, glass jars for perfume, the gold necklace and ornament. Also present are semi-precious stones, pearls, and uncut lumps of green aventurine quartz and lapis lazuli.

'How hard it is to enter the kingdom of God!'

The bright scarlet yarn catches the attention, with its end threaded through the needle's eye. Beneath are two camels, those massive beasts of burden. The saddle-cloth of one is richly decorated with blue and red patterns. Was it embroidered with this needle and thread? The absurd contrast of scale between a needle and the great creature wearing the saddle may make us smile—as no doubt Jesus intended his hearers to.

As on other occasions, a difficult piece of teaching is developed further, in private, with the disciples. Jesus is continuing to open their eyes to the cost of discipleship: everyone finds it difficult to abandon self-reliance and to throw themselves unreservedly on the mercy of God; but how much more difficult this is for rich people. To emphasize the point, Jesus uses one of his typically exaggerated, but very memorable, word-pictures. The disciples take the point, and begin to wonder at the futility of hoping ever to enter the kingdom.

That brings them to a moment of perception: humanly speaking, the enterprise they have set out on is impossible; it does actually all depend upon God.

Peter remarks that he and the other disciples have in fact taken the step the rich young man was unable to take. (And we remember from earlier in the Gospel that they had left home, family and livelihood, in order to follow.) Whereupon Jesus makes one of the most affirmative statements that we have yet heard him make to the disciples: there will be rewards for those who have had to leave family or property in order to follow him—in the form of a multitude of new relationships in the new community. It seems that they really are on their way into the kingdom.

But then Jesus quotes a proverb, by way of warning: the disciples may be amongst the first to be called, but they must not count on being first in the kingdom. As we shall be shown (on the next page), they were far from seeing clearly yet.

■ *camel* The Arabian camel or dromedary, *Camelus dromedarius*, is the largest living creature native to Palestine. A camel can stand up to two metres tall at the shoulder.
■ *for . . . the gospel* The word 'gospel' seems unlikely on the lips of Jesus, for it is a post-resurrection church word. Moreover, there are other signs of comment arising out of later Christians' experience in the phrase 'and with them, persecutions'. So it is probable that we are reading in this paragraph not only a record of Jesus' words, but also a little commentary upon those words by a very early Christian. The commentary will have encouraged early readers who were suffering for their Christian faith.

James and John request seats of honour

For the third time, the gospel text is written on the cross—this time more darkly grained than ever. It seems as though the cross is being plunged into deep billowing water, symbolically reflecting this page's teaching about baptism.

For the first time we are clearly informed that the goal of the journey, started some chapters ago, is to be none other than Jerusalem (which we have been led to suppose was a central source of suspicion and opposition to Jesus. There is a hint of a strange sense of apprehension in the first sentence: Jesus is leading the way, the disciples are astonished (although we are not told why), and other followers are afraid. The first readers will have empathized with those other followers, for in their own attempts to follow Jesus they knew well the physical risks of persecution.

These risks are now spelled out more clearly than ever before in Jesus' third prediction of his suffering. The message is much the same as before (see pages 54 and 59), but the detail is sharper: it will happen in Jerusalem, at the hands of 'the Gentiles' (that is, the Romans); he will be mocked, spat upon and flogged before being killed. We have by now grown used to the disciples' lack of understanding, so we are not surprised to find that the very next story follows the pattern set with the two earlier predictions. The first time Peter 'rebuked' Jesus; the second time they had argued about who was the greatest. And this time James and John try to manipulate Jesus into giving them high status when the kingdom arrives. In typical style, Jesus asks a further question in veiled language, trips the brothers up in their arrogant answer, and through it opens their eyes to the suffering in store for them.

Finally, we are given a highly significant interpretation of Jesus' own role: he will exercise his greatness through being a servant and will give up his life as 'a ransom for many'. This highly condensed phrase hints at the meaning given by Christians to Jesus' death.

■ *drink the cup* This is a poetic allusion to a painful destiny in store, as the quotation from Psalm 75 illustrates. The allusion will not have been lost on early Christian readers, who will have known that James did in fact suffer a violent death at the hands of Herod Agrippa in (or just after) 41CE (see Acts 12:2).
■ *be baptised* The first readers will quickly have caught an allusion to their own baptism. All followers of Jesus were baptised by immersion in water, and this was understood as a sharing in Christ's death and resurrection, through a symbolic drowning and restoration to dry land (see Romans 6:3–4). Willingness to enter into this death was the cost of following.

Blind Bartimaeus receives his sight

The scene is just outside Jericho's gateway, where the blind beggar Bartimaeus usually sits. But today, neither he nor anyone else is to be seen. Only his crumpled cloak lies there—in the spot where he threw it aside when he heard that Jesus was calling him.

This is the last healing story to be narrated in the Gospel, and it is significant in a number of ways: its location, the title given to Jesus, and the emphasis on the beggar's behaviour.

Readers with awareness of Palestine's geography would know that Jericho was the last large town through which you would pass, if you were approaching Jerusalem from the east. This Jericho story seems therefore to have been very appropriately placed here as a kind of bridge to what follows: for all the following events take place in Jerusalem. The story simultaneously closes the section which began with the account of another blind man being healed (page 53), and then (as we have noticed) continued with stories of the disciples' blindness.

'Son of David' is a surprising way to address Jesus—a title we have not heard before. We need not suppose that Bartimaeus knew anything about Jesus' ancestry. Rather, whatever it was that he had picked up about Jesus of Nazareth, he understood him to be someone of national, and perhaps nationalistic, importance. King David of old had been the first king of ancient Judah who reigned from Jerusalem—a city which he captured from the Canaanites and made his capital. So, in calling Jesus 'Son of David', Bartimaeus is saying a highly political thing. Publicly, loudly, and despite the people's rebuke, Bartimaeus is (as it were) heralding the new 'David', as he sets out on the last leg of his journey up to Jerusalem.

So the story is telling us an astonishing thing. Whereas for over two chapters the disciples who have closely accompanied Jesus have failed to see clearly who Jesus was, here is a simple beggar who despite his physical blindness has nevertheless recognized Jesus. So Bartimaeus symbolically stands for every Christian who has come to recognize Jesus. That seems to be why so much attention in the story is paid to the beggar's behaviour, for it mirrors the path into Christian faith: while blind (in spiritual darkness), he hears of Jesus; despite opposition from friends, he prays for mercy; on hearing that he was called, in a gesture of delight and commitment, he throws aside his only worldly possession and comes to Jesus; once in his presence, he asks for the thing he most wants—enlightenment; his request is granted, and he follows Jesus along the road of (Christian) discipleship. We, the readers, are being invited to do the same.

Jesus enters Jerusalem to popular acclamation

The sight the disciples might have seen as they followed Jesus' strange instructions for finding a mount. They had tramped across the open countryside to the village, and there, right beside the doorway to the first house was a young donkey, tied to a tethering ring. Its back bears no signs of being saddle-worn. As they stretched out their hands to untie the rope from the ring, did they wonder how Jesus' strange instructions had been so easily followed? The palm and olive branches above hint at the ecstatic scene ahead.

Everything in the Gospel so far leads us to believe that some kind of climax is about to happen. The previous page prepared us to see that Jesus (the 'new David') was about to enter the capital city. Now that Jesus and his followers are actually approaching Jerusalem, the atmosphere is full of anticipation—how will he be received as he enters the city?

The story implies that by deliberate forethought, Jesus stage-managed a public demonstration and through it made a highly significant claim without even speaking a word. He did so by choosing to enter the city riding on a mount, and not on foot (in the usual pilgrim fashion). And the mount he chose was a donkey. All these details have meanings which were immediately obvious to both the crowd at the time and to the first Christian readers of the story.

The meaning was clear to them because they were well familiar with a famous prophecy of Zechariah, which is here quoted in the left margin. Before their very eyes, the crowd was seeing this ancient prophecy being enacted. Was the rest of the prophecy about to be fulfilled too? There seemed to be highly political overtones to Jesus' silent action. The crowd caught the point and immediately broke into an ecstatic welcome fit for a king.

■ *Hosanna* A transliteration of a Hebrew word meaning 'Save now'. As the quotations in the right margin indicate (where it is translated 'save' or 'help'), it was an ancient form of address to God, or to the king. In spreading their cloaks and shouting this word, the crowd were acknowledging Jesus' silent claim.

Jesus curses a fig-tree near Jerusalem

A view of the city after walking from Bethany across the Mount of Olives, and on down into the valley separating it from Jerusalem. Small dwellings cling to the steep slope leading up to the city, with the temple astride the highest ground. A fig-tree, covered with rich foliage, stands by the roadside. Why should Jesus have expected to find fruit on it out of season?

This story, and its sequel (on page 70), is one of the strangest in the whole Gospel. It was unreasonable to try to pick fruit when 'it was not the season for figs', and the whole story seems largely out of character with the picture of Jesus presented in the rest of the Gospel. (Consequently, many scholars have supposed that the story is not reliable as a description of an actual historical event.)

Why, then, did the evangelist include this story in his Gospel? He has given us a clue to its interpretation by the way he tells it to us. It is in two parts (of which this page is the first); and in between the two parts he wedges a story about the temple (see the next page). This leads us to suppose that the story of the fig-tree and the story about the temple are to be interpreted alongside each other: each sheds light on the other—as we shall see on the next two pages.

In fact, the story of the fig-tree may be treated as an allegory about the Jews. If this sounds strange to modern ears, it would be less so to the first readers, for they knew very well that the scriptures often likened Israel to a vine or a fig-tree. The connection between the Jeremiah prophecy (in the left margin) and the fig-tree story is particularly striking.

■ *fig-tree* This species, *Ficus carica*, is still common around Jerusalem today. It comes into leaf in late March but does not usually bear edible fruit until about June. The Gospel presents all the narrative from chapter 11 onwards as happening in the Passover season—that is, in March/April.

Jesus drives merchants from the Temple

A scene of chaos and confusion. Cage doors open, doves flapping everywhere, tables overturned, money scattered all over the pavement. What kind of violent action lies behind this scene? What intense feeling motivated it?

The whole Gospel has been leading up to this climactic confrontation. From the beginning, we have been made aware of the opposition of Jerusalem's religious leaders. Now at last, arriving at the sacred temple himself, Jesus passes dramatic judgment upon its practice of religion. He seems to have been offended by the market-stall atmosphere caused by the need to change foreign pilgrims' money to local currency, with which they could pay their temple tribute and purchase birds for sacrifice. Quoting a prophecy from Isaiah (right margin), he claims that the outer court should be reserved as a place of prayer for Gentiles. The first Christian readers, mindful of scriptural prophecies concerning the temple (left margin), will have understood Jesus' action as a divine judgment against the whole temple sacrificial system and a sign that the kingdom of God was dawning.

■ *the temple area* A vast enclosure within the city, measuring about three hundred metres by five hundred metres. It was entered by many elaborate gateways and surrounded by colonnades. In the centre of the enclosure, on higher ground, stood the roofed shrine building containing an inner room called 'the Holy of Holies'. Immediately outside the shrine was a great stone altar, upon which was the sacrificial fire; throughout the day, priests were offering the animals brought by worshippers as burnt offerings (holocausts). The higher ground containing this shrine, altar, and two small adjacent courts, was surrounded by a stone fence. Gentiles were welcome to enter the general enclosure (the Court of Gentiles), but were forbidden, on pain of death, to pass through the inner stone fence; the inner courts were open to Jews only. The incident recounted on this page must have happened in the outer Court of Gentiles. The whole enclosure still exists in Jerusalem today, although none of the ancient buildings survive. Now known as the *Haram esh-Sharif* (the Noble Sanctuary), the area is a sacred Muslim site containing the Dome of the Rock and the Aqsa Mosque.

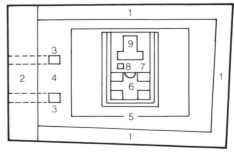

Temple enclosure

1 Colonnades
2 Royal colonnade
3 Subways to lower city
4 Court of Gentiles
5 Stone fence
6 Court of women
7 Court of Israel
8 Altar
9 Temple

The fig-tree and the Temple

This page seems to be a kind of fantasy. We have come down the Mount of Olives to exactly the same spot in the road as page 68. The same little house is still ahead of us. The fig-tree is in the same place as before, but leafless. Then fantasy takes over. For instead of facing the great slope up to the temple, the earth's surface seems to have opened, so that the sea has invaded the land. And the Temple Mount has vanished beneath the water.

The previous page's account of Jesus' violent judgment upon the temple—and perhaps also upon its sacrificial system of worship—helps in understanding this second part of the fig-tree story. In allegorical terms, the fig-tree seems to represent the temple and the religion it stood for. Like the tree with its leaves, traditional temple religion made a fine show of outward observances; but when Jesus came looking for the fruit of righteousness, he found none; as the tree was cursed and withered, so divine judgment would descend upon the temple. If it is right to interpret the story allegorically, its meaning will be something of this sort.

If so, there is a connection with the next saying about 'this mountain'. The phrase is very definite, as though Jesus was pointing to the Temple Mount as he said it. If that was the case, Jesus may have been teaching that it was possible to have faith in God without reference to temple rituals.

In early Christianity, there was dispute from the beginning as to whether Christians were obliged to keep Jewish ritual laws. Many Christians who were Jews by birth considered that the scriptures required this; but Gentile Christians considered themselves free of these obligations. Both groups would read with interest about Jesus' own attitude to the temple. The impression of his attitude which one gains from this Gospel is ambiguous: Jesus deliberately attends the temple and teaches there, but there is never any mention of his offering sacrifice there.

Jesus' authority is challenged in the Temple

The court in front of the central shrine of the temple. Normally it would be thronged with crowds of people waiting to make their sacrifices. Maybe it was here that the priests and teachers of the Law and elders challenged Jesus—in this very public place and in front of all the crowd.

Jesus' confrontation with the established leaders of Jewish religion increases in tempo. In the next few pages, he is shown to be in heated verbal controversy over particular matters of religion. First, he is publicly challenged over his authority to be 'doing these things'—which seems to refer to his violent action in driving out the temple merchants (page 69).

He answers in a typically rabbinic manner, by asking a further question. The supposition was that if they could answer the second question, they would also have answered their own question. But his choice of question is subtle, and through it he succeeds in outwitting the temple authorities. By challenging him in public, they may have hoped to humiliate him before the people; but in the end, it is the authorities themselves who are made to look foolish.

This confrontation helped confirm readers in the belief that Jesus' earlier action in expelling the merchants was indeed done with authority from God (that is to say, 'from heaven'). Many centuries earlier, the prophet Jeremiah had stood in the temple and in the name of God had proclaimed how it needed to be reformed (see the left margin of page 69). For this he was arrested and questioned (see the margin on this page). The earliest readers of the Gospel will have been aware with apprehensive anticipation of the parallels between the actions and fate of the ancient prophet, and those of Jesus.

The perspective of the illustration is as seen from the centre of the Court of Women, facing the steps leading up to the huge Gate of Nicanor. Its double gates made of bronze were over fifteen metres high and so heavy that it took a dozen priests to close them each evening. Behind, the facade of the shrine building rose to an imposing height of forty-five metres. The proportions throughout were massive, designed to overawe the worshipper; the doors were overlaid with gold and silver plates, as was the facade of the shrine, so that in sunlight it shone with a dazzling brilliance, befitting the deity; but the interior was mysteriously hidden from view by enormous double curtains.

The parable of the vineyard and the tenants

Baskets of harvested grapes are piled beside the vat, ready to be pressed. A dry stone boundary wall surrounds the vineyard. A raised watchtower breaks the skyline. Some unpicked bunches still hang from nearby vines. It looks as though something has disturbed the farmer in the middle of his work.

Confrontation with the Jewish religious leaders has been steadily building up. Now in this parable it seems as though Jesus is offering veiled comment upon what was happening: certainly the first Christian readers will have read the parable as a kind of prophecy of the suffering in store for Jesus, which heightened the drama at this point in the gospel story. They will have treated the story as an allegory in which the vineyard stood for Israel (as it did in a very famous prophecy of Isaiah that is given in the right margin), or for the city Jerusalem. Its owner and planter is God; the tenants are the Jewish leaders; the rejected servants stand for the abused prophets of former times (see the left margin). This much is common enough in Jewish story-telling.

But the conclusion has a highly Christian twist to it: the owner's only son 'whom he loved' sounds like a direct allusion to the voice from the cloud (page 56) referring to Jesus. To Christians, knowing how the gospel story was going to end, the description of the son being killed and thrown out of the vineyard sounded just like the crucifixion and burial of Jesus outside the city wall. The addition of the quotation from Psalm 118 about a rejected building-stone being chosen as just the right stone for a corner capstone takes the allusion even further: Jesus is to be that rejected stone, and he will be elevated to highest prominence by the resurrection.

So this page gives the reader a hint of the story to follow and how it is to be understood.

■ *vineyard* Vineyards were usually planted on hillsides in open country, and they were surrounded by stone walls to keep out wild animals which might damage the vines. When the grapes were finally ripening, the watchtower was used as a lookout by labourers who would scare off birds. They might also sleep there overnight. To press the juice, baskets filled with grapes were stacked upon each other, and a heavy flat stone placed on the top. The juice oozed through the basketwork, and down into the pit or vat below, from which large portable earthenware vessels were filled.

Pharisees question Jesus about paying Roman poll-tax

The page is dominated by the imposing statues of two Caesars: Augustus Caesar stands in a commanding pose wearing his military breastplate, whereas Tiberius Caesar sits to dispense justice. Above are both sides of the coin mentioned in the text: a silver denarius bearing the likeness of Tiberius Caesar. They symbolize the power and domination of imperial Roman rule.

Immediately a new confrontation follows: a public question which had direct political implications. It was put by two groups who held opposite attitudes to the Romans: the Pharisees had settled for the status quo and compromised with the Roman rulers, while the Herodians may represent a nationalist group from Galilee who favoured defiant action. The chosen question was a trap: whichever way Jesus answered, it seems likely that he would offend one party and in doing so endanger his following and perhaps his life.

The question concerned a particular Roman poll-tax levied on inhabitants of Judea since 6CE. It had to be paid in Roman currency, bearing the emperor's head and inscription. When first introduced it had provoked an armed rebellion led by Judas the Galilean (see Acts 5:37); anti-Roman guerrilla warfare had continued ever since. Any public pronouncement about this tax was likely to be interpreted as either sedition or betrayal.

Jesus' response to the question was astute. He asked for a denarius; they produced one; all could see that it bore the emperor's name and as such was be regarded as his personal property; undeniably, he had a right to his own property. Moreover, by getting them to produce the coin, Jesus was implying 'since you have in your possession Caesar's coin, you already acknowledge his authority and therefore have an obligation to pay tax to him'. Thus Jesus outwitted his questioners.

Early Christian readers of this story who were Gentiles and favoured Roman rule will have been impressed that Jesus had said nothing illegal.

■ *denarius* A Roman silver coin, weighing 3.8 grams. According to a story in Matthew's Gospel (chapter 20) a denarius was a day's wage for a labourer. The specimen illustrated was circulating during Jesus' lifetime. Its obverse bears the head of Tiberius (who reigned 14–37CE), and the Latin inscription TI CAESAR DIVI AUG F AUGUSTUS, ('Tiberius Caesar Augustus, son of the divine Augustus'). Its reverse bears a seated figure of Peace holding an olive branch, and the inscription PONTIF MAXIM ('High Priest'). The coin thus proclaimed the divinity of the emperor—an idea highly offensive to Jews.

The drawings below are based on original Roman statues, now preserved in the Vatican Museum in Rome.

Sadducees question Jesus about resurrection

The illustrations depict visible evidence for Jewish beliefs about resurrection. Below, cut into the living rock of the Mount of Olives, are a series of monumental memorials and shaft tombs which Jesus will have seen. Above is an elaborately carved stone ossuary—a box designed to preserve the bones of a deceased person, keeping them together inside a tomb, ready for the resurrection. It is decorated with rosettes—symbols of eternal life. The Sadducees would not have agreed with such ideas.

Confrontation again: this time with yet another religious group—the Sadducees. Most of the aristocratic families of Jerusalem, amongst them highly influential priestly families, were Sadducees. So by publicly rebutting them, Jesus was provoking powerful opposition.

The Sadducees founded their beliefs on a smaller collection of scriptures than most other Jews: they only accepted the authority of the Pentateuch, the first five books of the Bible which were held to have been written under divine inspiration by Moses. They did not accept belief in resurrection because there is no direct reference to this doctrine within the Pentateuch. (Belief in resurrection only entered Judaism at a relatively late date, occurring for the first time in the book of Daniel—see bottom right margin.) Here, the Sadducees attempt to show the absurdity of belief in resurrection by recounting an imaginary case, where (in accordance with the Mosaic Law in Deuteronomy 25—see top left margin) one woman had been successively married to seven men. Jesus responds by affirming belief in resurrection: they are mistaken in supposing that resurrected life is a resumption of our present lifestyle; moreover, the very scriptures accepted by the Sadducees contain wording which allows (and perhaps demands) belief in resurrection. For in God's revelation of himself in Exodus 3 (see lower left margin), he says 'I am the God of Abraham . . . ', not 'I was the God of Abraham'. Everyone knew these patriarchs had died long before Moses' time, so the grammar of the sacred text seems to imply they are alive in some other existence.

The great rock monuments depicted in the lower margin stand in the Kidron Valley, at the foot of the Mount of Olives, just outside Jerusalem's walls. They were constructed by rich families as memorials to their deceased members in the first and second centuries before Christ. The burials themselves were in artificial 'caves' cut in the limestone rock beside the monuments. Each 'cave' would belong to one extended family and would contain many horizontal shafts (shown in the right margin) where the shrouded bodies were laid to rest. After the flesh had decomposed, the bones of each corpse were reverently gathered together and placed in a stone ossuary box, as depicted at the top of the page, to await the resurrection.

A teacher questions Jesus about the greatest commandment

The Gospel's text appears as though it is written upon a parchment scroll. The sacred Jewish scriptures were (and are) written upon scrolls of this kind. We are visibly reminded of how Jesus himself will have studied the sacred texts intensively, feeding his own prayerful reflection from these ancient sources.

Over the previous four pages, we have seen Jesus decisively answer priests and Pharisees and Sadducees. Now a teacher of the Law poses a question much discussed by Jewish rabbis: which is the single most important law in the *Torah* upon which all the rest of the *Torah* hinges? Jesus answers by bringing together two texts from Deuteronomy and Leviticus (top margin). The first, commonly called the *Shema*, forms part of the daily prayer of a devout Jew. By linking it to the Leviticus quotation, he implied a means of interpreting the *Shema*: that love of God and love of neighbour are inextricably interwoven.

This answer serves to highlight the heart of religion, as Jesus saw it. And the story goes on to emphasize how Jesus' reply delighted his questioner, who (to judge from his allusion to Hosea and Samuel—see bottom margin) seems to have belonged to that strand within Judaism which gave secondary importance to temple rituals. So one effect of the story is to emphasize that although great rifts are appearing between Jesus and various religious leaders over certain of his actions and practices, Jesus' teaching is essentially orthodox and faithful to Jewish scriptures.

Early Jewish Christian readers, surrounded by disputes with Jewish leaders and often expelled from synagogues for their beliefs, will have been pleased to note that Jesus' central teaching did not conflict with Judaism. Moreover, they will have appreciated knowing that Jesus considered that a Jewish teacher of the Law could be 'not far from the kingdom of God'.

Before the development of the codex (that is, a book with cut leaves, bound down one edge), all books were written on scrolls. These were made from finely prepared leather or parchment, sewn together into a single strip many metres long, and wound round two rods. The text was written in parallel columns down the width of the strip. To find a particular passage, the scroll had to be laid on a table, and slowly wound from one rod to the other, until the selected passage became visible. The earliest surviving complete biblical scroll contains the whole of the book of Isaiah; it is made from seventeen strips of leather sewn into a scroll over seven metres long, with fifty-four columns of writing. One of the most famous of the Dead Sea Scrolls, it was already over a century old when Jesus was alive; it is now on public display in the Shrine of the Scroll in Jerusalem.

Jesus criticises teachers of the Law

At the top of the page is a specially carved stone seat from a synagogue, like those mentioned by Jesus. Below is a corner of the Court of the Gentiles, where Jesus probably taught alongside other religious teachers. The covered colonnades surrounding the temple's great open enclosure provide shaded space where rabbis and their disciples would discuss religious doctrines. The expenditure of vast wealth upon architecture of such grandeur and scale emphasizes the high place given to religion in Jewish society.

The first saying seems to spring out of arguments as to whether or not the coming Messiah (the Christ) was to be a lineal descendant of King David. There were many scriptures (including those in Samuel and Isaiah 9 and 11) which gave the hope of a God-sent ruler, sitting on David's throne, who would bring peace. Jesus, however, seems to have wanted to distance himself from such a political hope. He quotes a verse from Psalm 110 (assumed by all at the time to have been composed by David), and offers a novel interpretation (see below) implying a divine origin for the Christ. Later Christian readers, believing that all Old Testament texts spoke of Christ, will not have found this logic difficult.

The second saying about teachers of the Law is very harsh and contrasts sharply with the friendly encounter on the previous page.

■ *teaching in the temple courts* Along the full width of the south edge of the temple enclosure, King Herod the Great had built the Royal Colonnade. It was perhaps the most daring architectural achievement in the world of its time, being conceived on a massive scale. Its 162 pillars, each over eight metres high, were arranged in four rows, thus producing three vast aisles about 250 metres long. The roofs, supported on columns which rested on the lower columns, were visible from many miles away. There was nothing like it in the Roman world. The Jewish historian Josephus, who had served as a priest in the temple, proudly declared that this colonnade was 'a structure more noteworthy than any under the sun'.

■ *The Lord said to my Lord* The original meaning of this expression was, 'God said to the king'. But in rabbinical fashion Jesus interprets the sacred words for his own purposes as meaning, 'God said to my Lord' (with a capital letter, and implying a divine figure).

■ *important seats in the synagogues* The stone seat carved from a single block of basalt and depicted at the top of the page was found by archaeologists in the synagogue at Chorazin, in Galilee. Although it was made over a century after Jesus' time, it gives an example of public display of worthiness in a synagogue. Its inscription reads: 'May Yudan son of Ishmael who made this hall and its staircase be remembered for good. As his reward, may he have a share with the righteous'.

A poor widow offers her last penny

Jewish worshippers entering the temple by the Huldah Gateway would see this magnificent domed ceiling above their heads. Its magnificence contrasts starkly with the almost worthless copper coins offered by the widow in this story. Similarly, the fabulous visible wealth of the temple contrasts with the poor widow's hidden wealth of spirit.

This touching story is the last in this section of the Gospel: very appropriately, it rounds off the long narrative recounting Jesus' active ministry. Through many earlier chapters, Jesus has been trying to get his followers to perceive the nature of self-surrender involved in discipleship, but without much obvious success. More recently he has confronted leaders who controlled the teaching and structures of institutional religion, often in a way that excluded the common people. Now, at the very end of his active ministry, a very poor woman crosses his path. She is not even one of his followers. But in her unselfconscious action, she exemplifies that all he has been teaching about discipleship. She has offered everything she had—her whole life.

This story is thus a most fitting bridge to the final section of the Gospel—for in it we shall hear the manner in which Jesus himself offered his whole life, in the same spirit of self-abandonment as the poor widow.

■ *very small copper coins* A loose paraphrase. The Greek text names the coins: as two *lepta*. They were tiny copper coins, the smallest Greek ones in circulation and almost worthless.

■ *worth only a fraction of a penny* A loose paraphrase again. The Greek text names a Roman coin: a *quadrans*. This was the Latin name for the smallest Roman coin in circulation. This detail may have been added for the benefit of readers in the West, unfamiliar with Eastern currency.

■ *all she had to live on* The Greek text is deliberately ambiguous and means both 'her whole livelihood' and 'her whole life'.

The upper illustration is based upon the damaged ornamentation on a domed vault underneath the Aqsa Mosque in Jerusalem. This vault is a surviving part of a monumental entrance to Herod's temple from the lower part of the city. A double gate admitted worshippers through the southern wall of the sacred enclosure, and then a stepped passage, or subway, led them up to the much higher level of the Court of the Gentiles. The illustrated dome was just inside the entrance gate. This 'subway' entrance was one of several, designed to facilitate the movement of many thousands of pilgrims during temple festivals.

Jesus prophesies the Temple's destruction

An impression of Jerusalem as seen from the Mount of Olives. The vast temple enclosure, taking up one sixth of the city's land space, is obviously its proudest feature. To contemplate its destruction was to contemplate the destruction of a whole community and a whole culture. Beneath, fragments of some magnificently decorated temple building found by archaeologists—visible evidence of Titus' destruction and a prophecy fulfilled.

Jesus has already come into sharp confrontation with the leaders of institutional religion; a climax is now reached with his prophecy that the temple would be destroyed. To Jews of the time this will have seemed a sacrilegious or even blasphemous thing to utter, and the remark was bound to lead to a showdown. Long ago, the prophet Jeremiah had uttered a similar prophecy and had suffered persecution for his words. Christian readers will have been intrigued to hear Jesus' prophecy, not only because it seemed to mark the great divide between Christianity and Judaism, but also because everyone knew that the Roman army did in fact besiege Jerusalem, and after two years succeeded in capturing it in 70CE. The entire city, including the fabulous temple, was systematically demolished and burned.

■ *the Temple* All the features mentioned on page 69 are illustrated here: the tall central shrine, built on the summit of the mountain; the outer Court of Gentiles, separated from the inner courts by a stone fence; the whole enclosure surrounded by covered colonnades, the most elaborate of which was the Royal Colonnade on the south (left) side; two subways leading out from the Court of Gentiles, underneath the Royal Colonnade through a double and a triple gateway to the lower city. Adjacent to the enclosure on the north (right) side stands the Roman garrison's Antonia fortress, with its four towers. On the far side of the city, opposite the Royal Colonnade, Herod's royal palace is marked by its elaborate towers. To the right of Herod's palace, just outside an angle of the city wall, an old quarry is visible—the site of Golgotha.

■ *What massive stones!* Some of the largest stones are still to be seen in situ in the foundations of the south-west (far left) corner of the enclosure. At this point, Herod had built a massive substructure on the slopes of the Temple Mount, so as to increase the size of the Court of Gentiles, by creating an artificial platform, level with the mountain top. The foundations of this substructure are so massive that they were left undisturbed by Titus' army: one enormous stone, measuring 1.85 metres by 7 metres, is estimated to weigh over a hundred tons. The Royal Colonnade was daringly built at the very edge of this artificial platform, which at the south-east corner was fifty-four metres above ground level. The spectacle of the Colonnade, built on the edge of Herod's man-made cliff, drew amazement from all who saw it.

The Last Days: a warning of the miseries preceding them

The remainder of this chapter, spreading over this and the next three pages, is different in character from anything else in the Gospel. It is contructed as a single long speech, in a style quite unlike anything we have heard so far. The language is full of strange imagery, which it would be inappropriate to illustrate in the realistic style of the rest of this book. So, to mark the distinctive character of this chapter, these pages have no illustrations.

Very appropriately, the whole speech takes place on the Mount of Olives (see previous page)—traditionally the expected site of the Last Judgment. And it is given privately to four named disciples, at a point in the story just before Jesus' death. So the speech bears some likeness to death-bed scenes in the scriptures, when great leaders (such as Jacob, Moses, Samuel or David) made a final inspired utterance about the future. Because of all this, the first Christian readers will have regarded this speech with particular attention—especially if they were reading it in the late sixties of the first century, when the full force of Roman military might was building up against Jewish freedom-fighters in Palestine. And those Christians who read it after 70CE will have felt that they were living at the end of an era, having witnessed the destruction of Israel and of the sacred temple.

What the long speech does is to plot a programme for the last days, in such a way that readers can spot where they are living within that programme. It follows a pattern already set by contemporary Jewish visionaries (see right margin). The overall effect is to indicate that the programme has already begun, and that the last days are just round the corner.

But first, there will be 'birth-pains'. The image of a woman in labour is a striking one: the pain is agonizing for a while, but it is the sign that new life is on the way. It was a figure of speech used centuries before by Jewish prophets (see left margin). It was also a part of the teaching of Paul, appearing in his letter to the Thessalonians (written some two decades before this Gospel was compiled).

Early readers will have recognized that the 'birth-pains' had already begun: they had heard of wars (the Roman conquest of Britain in the West, and conflict with the Parthian empire in the East); there had been widespread famine under the emperor Claudius, who reigned 41–54CE (see Acts 11:28). They will also have recognized from their own experience the terror of persecution, arrest and trial described in the last two paragraphs. (The Acts of the Apostles is full of stories of such intimidation of Christians.) But through this period of 'birth-pains', the gospel will be proclaimed to all nations of the world.

The Last Days: the sign for knowing their arrival

The programme begun on the previous page continues with a description of a definite sign which will mark the arrival of the Last Days. But the passage is very obscure, and no one now knows precisely what the intended meaning was.

The reason why the passage is so difficult to interpret is that it is written in a code which was understandable to the original readers, but unfortunately the key to this code is now lost to us. The phrase 'the abomination that causes desolation' seems to be a secret way of speaking about some sacrilegious person or thing or event. And the curious phrase 'let the reader understand' seems to mean that at this point the church official reading the Gospel aloud was to break off and give an extemporary explanation of the phrase to the congregation.

What explanation might the reader have offered? It is certain that some allusion to the visions in the book of Daniel is intended, for the strange phrase 'abomination that causes desolation' comes straight out of that book. In Daniel, the phrase is a secret codified way of referring to a catastrophic event which happened in Jerusalem in 168BCE, when the pagan Greek ruler Antiochus Epiphanes profaned the temple in Jerusalem by building in it an altar (and perhaps also a statue) to Zeus (see 1 Maccabees 1:54). This event marked the beginning of a period of severe religious persecution in Judea. Daniel was written in this codified way for fear of rulers who would consider it treasonable.

It is possible that a similar act of profanation by a contemporary pagan ruler was in mind when this passage of the Gospel was written. Such a catastrophe very nearly occurred when the deranged Roman emperor Caligula ordered a statue of himself to be erected in the Jerusalem Temple in 40CE. (However, he was murdered before his order could be carried out.)

This passage will have been interpreted in different ways at different times, and adapted to local situations—particularly by the Christians living in Jerusalem. For the odd thing about the passage is that it does not speak about the end of the world but about a catastrophe which would happen in Judea, and maybe in winter. It seems that this very passage (or a Christian prophecy based directly on it) saved the Christian inhabitants of Jerusalem from the Romans: the historian Eusebius records that just before the Roman armies laid siege to the city in 68CE, the Christian community, acting on a prophecy, fled to safety across the River Jordan to the city of Pella.

The Last Days: the closing scene

These two paragraphs are the final stage of the programme begun two pages earlier— the climax to which the whole prophecy has been leading. The scene has shifted abruptly and unaccountably from a catastrophe in Judea to something on a cosmic scale: a terrifying picture of a general break-up of the universe, during which the Son of Man will appear and gather the 'elect', meaning chosen ones.

In a condensed form, the passage makes allusions to many scriptures. It had been common imagery in earlier prophecies to speak of the collapse of the heavens as a symbol of the wrath of God (left margin). So, not surprisingly, this imagery is repeated here.

The Son of Man imagery is drawn from the vision in Daniel 7 (right margin). This chapter became immensely important to Christians as a means of handling a deep paradox of their faith. On the one hand they knew that Jesus submitted himself to earthly rulers and was put to death by them. On the other hand they believed that Jesus had been sent by God, and that God's eternal power had not been overcome by the earthly rulers who executed Jesus. Even if this was not apparent to all their contemporaries at the moment, they believed there would come a time in the future when all humanity would recognize it—Jesus would come again with heavenly power, at the end of time.

Daniel 7, with its talk of a figure 'like a son of man' being given everlasting dominion by God, became an influential scripture in forming Christian thought about the paradoxical abasement and exaltation of Christ. Earlier in the Gospel, Jesus had predicted his coming suffering; and he did so in Son of Man language. Now the Son of Man imagery returns, but this time associated with power and glory.

This prophecy of ultimate triumph comes immediately before the story of Jesus' suffering, and so it affects the way in which this story is heard and understood. Indeed right in the middle of that story, during his trial, Jesus will make reference to the Son of Man coming in clouds (see page 89). The Christian belief in the ultimate exaltation of Christ is thus held up before readers as they embark upon the story of Jesus' sufferings.

Various sayings on watchfulness

These three paragraphs share a general purpose of encouraging Christian readers to be on the alert, waiting and watchful—ready for their 'owner's' return (as the last paragraph puts it).

But the various sayings do not closely relate to each other, probably because they were once quite separate utterances of Jesus: the sayings were remembered, but the original contexts forgotten. And now they are only linked by the editorial device of key phrases ('these things happening', 'at the door', 'pass away', 'watch').

This may explain why the saying 'No one knows about that day or hour' seems to some to be so out of keeping with the scheme laid out on the previous three pages. That programmatic scheme seemed to be designed to indicate whenabouts 'that day' might come, and to recognize that it was not far off. Now we are told it is known only to God. This seeming contradiction raises important questions for modern minds: on this view, how can Jesus have taught both of these things? How much of the teaching of this chapter actually comes from Jesus, and how much from the beliefs of early Christian communities?

Certainly some aspects of the programme on page 79 sound strange on Jesus' lips, for they speak very specifically of persecutions which happened to Christians after Jesus' lifetime. Moreover, the teaching that 'the Holy Spirit' would give them words to speak when on trial, while a common Christian way of speaking, is unusual coming from Jesus.

So some have thought it possible that portions of this chapter reflect post-resurrection Christian teaching rather than the pre-resurrection teaching of Jesus. Early Christians, however, will not have been interested in making these kind of distinctions. For them, the words of Jesus were living words, which the community adapted to new situations as time went by. They did not consider such adaptation to be deceptive, for they believed that the risen Christ continued to speak within his 'body', the church. During community worship it could happen that a member prophesied under inspiration of the Holy Spirit, giving a precise message to the community, as though the risen Lord were speaking to them directly. This may be the kind of context in which genuine sayings of Jesus were developed and expanded to apply to particular trials facing later Christians.

Early Christians facing such trials will have been greatly encouraged to feel that Jesus spoke of their situation, and indeed set them an example of how to watch (in Gethsemane), and how to bear themselves when arrested, when flogged, when on trial, and when answerable before a governor and a king. All these afflictions happen to Jesus in the story that follows.

The Passion Narrative begins

An alabaster perfume jar, the plant from which nard is manufactured, and a leather purse with silver coins. The first is a lavish sign of love, the last a reward for betrayal. The motives for both the love and the betrayal lie mysteriously hidden from us. And both are responses to the same person.

At this point the style of the Gospel changes again. For the first time we now encounter a connected narrative—a carefully organized account of a series of detailed events that happened over the short space of about five days. It all takes place in Jerusalem, at a particular season of the year, and names of people and localities are included. This part of the Gospel has come to be known as the Passion Narrative. ('Passion' is derived from the Latin *passio*, meaning 'suffering'.)

The Jewish feasts of Passover and of Unleavened Bread happened at the same time during a particular new moon, in March/April of the modern calendar. It was the most important festival of the year, commemorating the beginnings of the Jewish nation (see further on the next page). Jewish pilgrims would travel from distant lands in order to celebrate the feast in Jerusalem, thus swelling the population of the city to as much as a quarter of a million people. All the ingredients for a nationalistic riot were present, so the religious authorities were understandably anxious to avoid any unrest which might provoke Roman reprisals.

Once the general scene has been set, the Passion Narrative opens with an important symbolic action: Jesus is anointed on the head (like the kings of former days) by a woman. Later on, the Passion Narrative will end with women coming to his tomb to anoint his corpse—but not finding it. Greek-speaking readers, knowing that 'Christ' meant 'anointed one' in their language, will also have recognized that in opening the Passion Narrative this story provides a key to its interpretation—suffering even to the point of death is the mark of God's anointed one, 'the Christ'.

■ *Bethany* Long identified as the modern village of el-Azariyeh, on the eastern slope of the Mount of Olives, not quite two kilometres from Jerusalem.
■ *alabaster jar* Alabaster is a translucent form of gypsum; being stone it is not porous like pottery, and it was therefore used for storing precious fluids such as perfume. It would have been sealed with wax, and the narrow neck of the jar would have to be broken to extract the fluid.
■ *nard* A perfume manufactured from spikenard, *Nardostachys jatamansi*, a plant from which aromatic oil is obtained. It is native to the Himalayas, and so the perfume must have been imported by merchants from India, and would have been exceptionally expensive.
■ *money* The coins illustrated include *tetradrachmai*, silver currency minted in Tyre and commonly used in Judea at the time.

Preparations for the Passover meal

A table laden with the special food for a Passover feast: roast lamb, unleavened bread, bitter herbs, a sauce of fruit purée, and wine—each of them symbolic of an aspect of ancient Israel's deliverance from slavery.

This story bears some resemblance to the finding of the donkey (see page 67), and is probably also intended to emphasize Jesus' prophetic powers of foresight. While a man carrying a water jar would be an unusual sight (fetching water was women's work), there is no indication of a pre-arranged secret rendez-vous. Rather, the householder's willingness to be at the disposal of Jesus (just like the donkey owner's), seems to be a sign of divine control over this event, as over everything else in the Passion Narrative: nothing happens accidentally—everything that takes place is within God's pre-ordained will.

As the quotation from Deuteronomy (in the margins) makes plain, the food for this feast had symbolic significance. Over a thousand years before, when the Hebrews had been slaves in Egypt, on this very night each family had slaughtered a lamb, put its blood on their doorposts, and eaten a hasty meal. They had been dressed ready for a journey and were waiting for the right moment to make their escape. During the night the angel of God slaughtered the firstborn of each Egyptian household, but 'passed over' each household with blood on its doorposts; in the ensuing confusion, the Hebrews escaped and, under God's protection, marched through the desert towards the land of Israel; during their hasty flight they did not have time to bake bread properly, and made do with unleavened bread. (The whole story is recounted in Exodus 12.)

Jewish Christians will have had all of this knowledge at the back of their minds when they read this page and the next one. Moreover, the whole Passion Narrative which follows will have seemed parallel to the Passover story: in both cases a death was believed to have achieved freedom for a people. So an indirect interpretation of the meaning of Jesus' death is presented.

■ *eat the Passover* The Passover was celebrated at night on the fifteenth day of the month Nisan (called Abib in an earlier calendar). Its central feature was a communal meal at which a roasted lamb was eaten. These lambs had to be ritually slaughtered in the temple the previous afternoon, and the ensuing meal had to take place in Jerusalem or its immediate environs. The bitter herbs represented the bitterness of slavery, the sauce represented the clay from which the slaves made bricks and the wine was a symbol of new-found freedom in the Promised Land.

The Last Supper

A cup filled with wine, and a broken matzah *(unleavened bread): two elements of the traditional Jewish Passover feast to which Jesus added a new symbolic significance.*

No early Christian could read this page without bringing their experience of the Eucharist into their interpretation of it. Long before the Gospel was written, Paul was guiding the Christians in Corinth about their style of worship and passed on to them an account of the Last Supper remarkably close to the Gospel's account.

Many things must have taken place at this meal, but we are told only two. First, a snatch of conversation; second, a symbolic action.

The conversation about his impending betrayal shows that Judas' treachery does not take Jesus by surprise. He actually anticipates it (although without naming Judas). Moreover, through a subtle allusion to Psalm 41 (left margin), this treachery is seen as a necessary part of the divine plan, although it does not excuse Judas of responsibility for his actions.

The symbolic action echoes two stories we have heard earlier in the Gospel (pages 44 and 50), but adds a new element. In the earlier feasts with crowds, the same four-fold action (taking, thanking, breaking, giving) was observed; but now some startling new words are added: 'This is my body . . . this is my blood of the new covenant'. How may the first readers have understood these words?

In common with all ancient cultures, they will have felt that a sacred bond was formed between people who shared a meal together. (That was what made Judas' betrayal so terrible.) But this is no ordinary meal; it is the last meal Jesus is to share with his disciples. Thereafter his visible union with his followers will be broken until the kingdom of God came in its fulness (see the final sentence). For the interim period, Jesus is providing a means of invisible union with himself by investing a broken loaf and a shared cup of wine with special meaning. They will have understood him to be instituting a sacramental rite: all who ate the bread participated in his body, the church. And his blood, poured out like a sacrifice, inaugurated the 'new covenant' anticipated by Jeremiah (right margin); and all who drank the wine (both original disciples and later Christians) had a means of participating in the atoning effects of his sacrificial death.

■ *Then he took the cup* A ritual which took place at a particular point in the Passover meal. While holding the cup, a special thanksgiving prayer was said (left margin). Everyone then said 'Amen', and silently drank from the cup in turn. On this occasion, Jesus broke the silence with his special interpretative words.

Jesus foretells the disciples' desertion and Peter's denial

The full moon of Passover barely lights a track leading up the mountainside ahead of us. On either side are olive groves. The cross shape of this page's design anticipates a night spent wrestling with fear.

Psalm 116, one of the hymns traditionally sung at the end of a Passover meal, contains many resonances with what was about to happen. The meal over, they went outside the city wall to the neighbouring hillside (where no doubt many Passover pilgrims were camping out overnight, as the religious regulations required people to be in the environs of the city).

Jesus then makes two striking predictions. First, that the disciples will forsake him, and even deny knowing him. As we shall see shortly, it all happened just as he had foretold (see pages 88 and 90). Once again this seems to be a sign that we should not suppose that anything happened accidentally: even the betrayal and arrest of Jesus were within the divine purpose.

The second prediction is a surprising one: 'After I have risen, I will go ahead of you into Galilee'. It is also referred to later on (see page 96), even though its precise fulfilment is not recounted in the narrative. But just as the first prediction is soon shown to be exactly fulfilled, so we are led to hope that the second one will be too. In this way readers are encouraged to anticipate this hope, just at the moment when they enter a dark and threatening part of the story.

■ *Mount of Olives* This hill, already referred to on pages 67 and 78, lies immediately to the east of Jerusalem. Its summit rises higher then the Temple Mount, and from its slopes there is a panoramic view of the whole city. Its name suggests that it was planted with olive orchards.

The trees illustrated on this and the next page are olives, *Olea europaea*, which thrive on the poor soil of rocky hillsides. They can live to a great age, and may have trunks up to one metre in diameter.

Jesus prays in Gethsemane

Deep night, on the stony ground of an olive orchard, among ancient gnarled trees that have lived through several human generations. It is a place of quiet on the edge of a crowded city, a place to find one's true self.

After a busy day and a late-night feast, one might expect the remainder of the night to be spent sleeping. But Jesus stays awake, keeping watch, on vigil, praying. He expresses disappointment that the disciples do not do the same. This page seems to be giving us an account of how, in his last hours, Jesus lived out his own teaching on page 82: not knowing when 'the hour' of his testing would come, he kept watch, and prayed and was ready when 'the hour' suddenly arrived (see the last paragraph). By contrast, Peter and the others fell asleep and were taken by surprise. The first Christian readers, who knew the terror of state persecution, will have seen here an example of how to prepare for possible arrest—and how not to.

Twice before Jesus had selected Peter and James and John to accompany him. On both occasions they witnessed something special and mysterious: the dead restored to life, and Jesus appearing in divine glory and named as 'my Son'. So we might expect another special revelation at this point too. This is exactly what happens: we are given a unique insight into the inner strivings of Jesus' soul. Close to being overwhelmed, he prays to God—and does so with astonishing familiarity, using a very special word (see below). Christian readers cannot fail to have recognized that Jesus was in effect praying 'the Lord's Prayer' (left margin). So the special revelation is the paradox that the transfigured Son in glory must also drink 'the cup' of suffering and death.

■ *Gethsemane* A very precisely named locality. The name in Aramaic means 'oil press', a most appropriate name for a spot on the Mount of Olives. Modern pilgrims can visit a walled garden containing some exceptionally old olive trees. It is on the lower slopes of the Mount of Olives, just at the point where the old road from Jerusalem to Jericho begins to ascend. Foundations of a fourth-century church on the site indicate that Christian pilgrims have come to pray at this particular place since at least that time.
■ *Abba* An Aramaic word, used by children in addressing their father. The word will have sounded as strange to Greek-speaking readers as it does to modern ears. But the fact that this 'foreign' word was preserved in the gospel text suggests that it was the actual word with which Jesus habitually addressed God in prayer. Twice Paul refers to *Abba* being used by Christians in prayer (see Romans 8:15 and Galatians 4:6); this seems to indicate that the first Christians copied Jesus' address to God, even if they did not (like him) speak Aramaic.

Jesus is arrested

A page in dark tones, with a menacing feel about it. A short sword and rough club hint at a readiness for violence; a linen garment discarded at the foot of an olive tree witnesses to a narrow escape. How can it be that a man once thronged by crowds was deserted in his hour of need?

The account of Jesus' arrest is told simply enough, although the first readers will have been impressed by several aspects of it.

First, a theological conundrum which lies within the story: the arrest came about through the deliberate act of one man, but also because 'the Scriptures must be fulfilled'. Judas' choice of sign suggests a hideously deceptive character, devoid of feeling; yet his kiss enabled the divine plan of salvation to proceed. The narrative only tells the story and leaves the reader to ponder unaided.

Second, Jesus personally offers no resistance. If he was later accused of stirring up political unrest, he roundly denies it here by both word and action.

Third, Jesus' own prophecy that he would be forsaken (see page 86) is seen to be fulfilled already. This has the effect of suggesting that he is strangely in charge of events, even though he appears to be the one with least power.

Fourth, there is a hint that a particular eye-witness was present, who later testified within the earliest Christian community of Jerusalem as to what happened that night. The curious reference to the anonymous lad who bravely followed, and so narrowly escaped capture, may imply that this young man lived to tell his tale afterwards within the Christian circle—and everyone in that circle would know just who it was who fled away naked!

Jesus on trial before the Jewish high priest

The log fire, burning through the night in the high priest's courtyard. A shocked and shivering Peter, bravely following 'at a distance', may have stared into its depths as he sought warmth and anonymity. Meanwhile, inside, a fiery trial was proceeding.

In many respects this page is the climax towards which the whole story has been leading. Earlier on, we have had hints from the words of demons and of Peter that Jesus was 'the Christ'; but these claims were always silenced by Jesus. But now, for the first and only time, Jesus publicly acknowledges the title 'the Christ'. And he does so quite plainly before the highest court of the Jewish people. This was very important to the first Christian readers: it gave them the impression that the Jews (through their appointed leaders) had stubbornly and deliberately refused to recognize their Messiah, even when he had revealed himself openly.

Moreover, a further impression is gained that the proceedings involved an attempted perversion of justice—although no criminal evidence was successfully produced. In the end, the charge is shown to have been one of blasphemy, as Jesus applies the Son of Man imagery of the Book of Daniel to himself. In fact, however, it is not clear that technical blasphemy was committed, for Jesus (just as much as the high priest) deliberately avoids taking the divine name upon his lips (see below).

The gospel text leaves us with an overriding impression that the initiative for Jesus' death rested firmly with the Jews (although in the end he was executed by Romans). Early Christian readers used this evidence when presenting the story of the crucifixion to pagan Romans—it served to reduce the blame which might be attached to the Roman authorities for having executed Christ.

And once again, everything seems to happen in accordance with scripture (as the marginal quotations suggest).

■ *Sanhedrin* The Jewish council with supreme judicial authority. Meeting under the presidency of the high priest, its seventy-one members included the heads of the great priestly families, the teachers of the Law, and lay elders.
■ *the Blessed One/the Mighty One* Indirect phrases used by Jews to avoid uttering the divine name (and thus avoid an accidental lapse into blasphemy).

With the hindsight of centuries, the anti-Jewish bias of the account on this page must be seen as regrettable. This passage, and others like it, became the basis of anti-Semitic propaganda, resulting in the deaths of countless Jews in later persecutions by Christians—although, of course, no such intention was in the mind of the gospel writer.

Peter denies knowing Jesus

Perched on a high vantage point, a cock raises its head to herald the dawn of a new day. Nature instinctively pursues its normal course on a day which, for Peter, opens so shamefully. Nevertheless, it was a day which future generations were to call Good Friday.

The story seems to be writing itself. On page 86, Jesus had prophesied to Peter 'tonight . . . before the cock crows twice you yourself will disown me three times'. And now it all happens, just as Jesus had foreseen. So the story continues with the strange sense (noted before) that Jesus the powerless prisoner is the one in control of events.

The story of Peter's denial is deliberately intertwined with the account of Jesus' trial. The effect is that two contrasting trials seem to be going on at the same moment: Peter's trial takes place informally in the courtyard, while Jesus' trial proceeds inside the high priest's house. Early readers, who themselves risked arrest and trial for their Christian faith, will have drawn some lessons from this story.

They will have noticed how Jesus, true to the teaching of chapter 13, stayed awake, watching prayerfully, preparing himself for his hour of testing; by contrast, Peter fell asleep (see page 87). Subsequently Jesus faithfully bears his witness before the council (Sanhedrin), setting an example for the situation mentioned on page 79. By contrast, Peter, challenged by a mere servant girl, denies even knowing Jesus and withdraws ignominiously to the shadows: he has not 'kept watch', and is not ready when the cock crows.

So the story will have been read by early Christians as a warning to themselves: under pressure, they too might very easily deny Christ. However, there was hope in the story too; for everyone knew that later on Peter became a great leader of the church, and had recently been witnessing faithfully to Christ in Rome, where he had died as a martyr. So Christian readers who had given way under cross-questioning had no need to despair.

■ *cock* The bird illustrated is the jungle fowl, *Gallus domesticus*, the ancestor of the modern domestic fowl. Cocks in the first century would probably have looked like this.

Jesus on trial before Roman authorities

A page emphasizing the immense power of Roman rule and the ruthlessness with which it could be imposed. At the foot of the page the Antonia fortress, a barracks for Roman troops, towers over city dwellings. It is strategically positioned, abutting the temple enclosure itself. Jesus may have been tried within this building. On the right is a whip with several leather thongs, each barbed with pieces of bone and lead. On the left are the remains of an inscription bearing the name of Pilate (Pilatus). That Jesus suffered crucifixion under Pontius Pilate is a universally accepted and irrefutable historical fact about his life.

Everyone knew that crucifixion was a specifically Roman form of execution, reserved for the basest criminals and slaves. What had Jesus done to deserve such a sentence? People living under Roman government would be unlikely to pay attention to the Christian message without having a satisfying answer to this question. So the account of Jesus' trial before a Roman authority was crucial.

The text is at pains to indicate that Pilate finds no fault with Jesus. In fact there is no mention at all of any formal sentencing. On the contrary, Pilate clearly does not believe the priests' charge, perceives that their motive was 'out of envy', and attempts to appeal over their heads to the crowd. But his ploy does not work; the priests stir up the people, and Pilate is forced to avoid a riot by giving way to their demands—a miscarriage of justice, perhaps, but (in Roman eyes) an excusable expedient for keeping the peace.

Thus the text represents the real responsibility for Jesus' death as resting with the Jews (and not the Romans). And the public charge is the alleged claim to be 'king of the Jews'—a political claim which the earlier gospel stories have shown Jesus had tried to avoid. Nevertheless, his ambiguous reply to Pilate neither confirms nor denies the kingly title.

■ *Pilate* The fifth procurator of Judea, in office from 26CE to 36CE. He was described in a contemporary letter as an 'inflexible, merciless, and obstinate' man, continually given to corruption, violence and cruelty of every kind. Eventually the emperor removed him from office for his tactless style of governing. The fragmentary inscription (found by archaeologists in Caesarea) appears to be a dedication stone of a public building declaring: . . . *Tiberieum* (*Pon*)*tius Pilatus* (*Praef*)*ectus Iuda*(*ea*)*e*, 'Pontius Pilate prefect of Judea (has dedicated) a temple in honour of Tiberius'. The Jewish historian Josephus' brief note about Jesus' being condemned to crucifixion by Pilate is independent evidence, confirming the Gospel's account. The mention of Pilate's name in the text is the only piece of information in the entire Gospel which links the story with the rest of world history in a way that is clearly datable.

Jesus is mistreated as a mock king

The instruments of humiliation: a length of purple cloth for his body, a coronet of plaited thorns for his head, and a stout stick for beating. With these, the Roman soldiers derisively mistreat Jesus, in mocking pretence of homage—as though he were the divine emperor Augustus (depicted on the coin above).

The theme of kingship is taken up again, this time in mocking derision. The Roman soldiers humiliate their prisoner by pretending to take his alleged kingly status seriously. Familiar with the public honours due to their emperor, they dress him in purple (a colour reserved for the emperor), improvise a crown, and offer a loyal subject's greeting—then exercise their power, and beat him about the head. The homage 'Hail, King of the Jews!' seems to be a parody of the Roman homage *Ave Caesar Imperator*, 'Hail, Imperial Caesar!'.

The first Christian readers will have sensed a high degree of irony in the scene. For to them the soldiers will have seemed to have acted more truly than they knew— since in their belief Jesus was indeed king, supreme even over Caesar.

As attentive readers, we are not taken by surprise by this part of the Passion Narrative. For several chapters ago (page 65) we read how Jesus had clearly predicted that he would be handed over to the Gentiles, who would mock him, spit on him, flog him and kill him. Now it is all happening just as he said.

■ *Praetorium* A Latin word, here apparently meaning the official residence of the Roman governor.

■ *crown of thorns* The thorny crown may not have been intended as an instrument of torture so much as a mock symbol of kingly or imperial dignity, and may be related to the way the divinized emperor Augustus was depicted. After his death, Augustus was declared 'divine', and his successor Tiberius issued the illustrated coin in his honour. The inscription reads *Divus Augustus Pater*, 'Divine Father Augustus'. The circlet on his head is intended to look like radiant divine glory, although the 'spikes' resemble thorns. This coin, a *dupondius*, was circulating in Rome from 22CE onwards, which means it was used during Jesus' lifetime.

Jesus is crucified

At the foot of the cross we see the executioners' tools and dice, Jesus' discarded clothes, and the drugged wine. On earlier pages foretelling Jesus' death, we have seen the cross shaft—but never so dark as here. The battered wedges securing its base seem to speak of the horrific violence of this brutal form of execution.

The fact of the crucifixion is given, with the utmost simplicity, in a single sentence. Significantly, there is no stress whatever upon the torture or the suffering inflicted on Jesus, nor on his manner of bearing it. However, a number of other details are included: he is offered drugged wine, but refuses it; his clothing is divided by casting lots; the written charge is stated; he is crucified between two robbers; bystanders hurl mocking insults at him. Why were these details included, while descriptions of his physical suffering were not? The answer seems to be that the first readers did not need an account of the suffering—they had witnessed the horrific sight of crucifixions often enough. What they did need was some account of why this terrible execution was necessary—and the recorded details each help to supply the reason: it all happened according to the will of God, even the little details being foretold in the ancient scriptures (especially Isaiah 53 and Psalm 22). Comparison of the Passion Narrative with the marginal quotations on this page and the next are particularly striking. The effect of the wording of the title is ironic: while intended as an accusation, it actually declares what the first Christians believed. Silently it appealed to the people, and vocally the Jewish leaders derisively rejected its claim. In later years Christians were to have the greatest difficulty in preaching the cross to Jews, but the Passion Narrative shows that the cross was an offensive stumbling-block to faith from the beginning.

■ *Golgotha* An Aramaic word, meaning 'skull'. It seems to describe a very particular location, known to Jerusalemites. Modern visitors to the Church of the Holy Sepulchre in Jerusalem are shown a chapel raised up above ground level, which has been regarded as the site of the crucifixion since at least the fourth century. Recent excavations have demonstrated that this chapel is not artificially raised up but rests on a protruding lump of bedrock; moreover, the bedrock under the rest of the church shows itself to have been an ancient quarry. From this evidence it is possible to reconstruct the probable landscape of Golgotha and its surroundings: a disused quarry, beside the road leading to a gateway in the western city wall; within the quarry a hump of rock left unquarried because its stone had weaknesses. This isolated hump, which perhaps looked like a gigantic skull, proved a good site to execute criminals in full sight of the road and city wall. All of this accords well with the description of typical crucifixion sites given by the Roman writer Quintilian.

The death of Jesus

A cross-shaped design: the text forms the lower part of the shaft, and a wine-soaked sponge is held up to the head of the cross, which is as black as the darkness over the land; the cross-beam is represented by the curtain of the temple torn in two from top to bottom. The black darkness and the reddened sponge seem to speak of the hideousness of violent death; yet the horror of them seems to be softened by the dignified nobility of the curtain—just as horror and nobility are both present in the story.

The Passion Narrative records only one piece of information as to the manner of Jesus' dying: he died with a question on his lips: 'Why . . . ?' If he was (mistakenly) thought to be summoning Elijah to his assistance, nothing happens. And he expires, his question unanswered.

However, Christian readers will instantly have recognized that these last words of Jesus are actually the opening words of Psalm 22—a psalm already much referred to in the Passion Narrative. The giving of the vinegar drink was in accordance with this ancient scripture, and so were the words of Jesus' anguished question. In this way the Passion Narrative refuses to minimize the horror of Jesus' death by crucifixion, and at the same time it quietly implies that even the anguish is within the will of God and achieves God's purpose.

The significance of Jesus' death is instantly shown in the Narrative through two happenings. First, the curtain of the temple is ripped open. This seems to refer to the great curtain inside the temple shrine which kept the interior hidden from public view (see page 71). Only priests were permitted to pass through the curtain into the shrine, which contained an inner room representing the presence of God—a place into which no ordinary Jew would dare venture. But the Narrative implies that the curtain being torn, the way into God's very presence lies open—the barrier that was so strongly emphasized by Jewish religion has been overcome by Jesus' death. The Jewish temple with its sacrificial system has been superseded as a way to God. That, it seems, is the first significance attached to Jesus' death.

The second significance concerns the Gentile world, and is shown through the Roman centurion's words. He becomes the first person, and a Gentile at that, to be brought to belief in the divine sonship of Jesus. And it is precisely through Jesus' death that he comes to this realization. He thus becomes the prototype of all later Christians (including this Gospel's readers) who would come to faith through Christian preaching about the cross.

The final paragraph notes that a number of women were present at Jesus' death, and three of them are named. They will be important witnesses to all that follows.

The burial of Jesus

A colourless page, drained of life. A new linen shroud lies on the rock slab to receive the corpse. Then, the hasty burial over, there is a last look back down the rock-cut steps to the tomb. The great round stone has been rolled out of its niche and firmly blocks any intruders.

The Roman practice was to leave crucified corpses on their crosses until they rotted or were eaten by birds, as the quotation from the Roman poet Juvenal in the right margin explains. This was highly offensive to Jews, whose law required executed criminals to be buried the day they died (see left margin). Accordingly, Jesus' body was removed from the cross and buried. The initiative for doing this came from a prominent councillor, who (the text implies) was a wealthy man. Thus in yet another detail, the events surrounding Jesus' death conform to the prophecy in Isaiah 53.

■ *a tomb cut out of rock* Ancient rock-cut tombs survive all around Jerusalem. The text seems to refer to a particular design of tomb approached by several steps cut down a couple of metres into the bedrock: at the foot of the steps was a low doorway which led into the tomb itself; one would have to stoop or enter on hands and knees; inside was the rock shelf on which the body was laid out, wrapped in its grave-clothes; the low doorway could be closed by rolling a heavy round stone (like a millstone) out of its specially cut niche at the foot of the steps.

In 326ce the emperor Constantine built an elaborate monument to protect the tomb traditionally regarded as the burial place of Jesus. The rock shelf still survives inside the present Church of the Holy Sepulchre. A few metres away are remains of other ancient rock tombs. This seems to demonstrate that the church is indeed built on an ancient cemetery. There is no good reason to doubt that the first Christians of Jerusalem correctly remembered the tomb in which their Lord had been laid, and that local oral tradition accurately transmitted this information through the six or so generations of memory between Jesus and Constantine.

Section and plan of typical rock-cut tomb

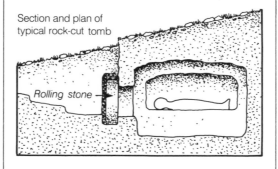

Rolling stone

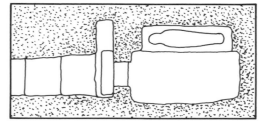

Three women visit the tomb

The only page illustrated with a photograph: dawn over the Sea of Galilee. This final page serves to link a story from long ago with the reader's own time. From the beginning, Christians claimed that the world's history had taken a different shape simply because Jesus had lived: the kingdom of God had dawned on that first Easter Day.

The previous page has described how, because of the approaching sabbath, Jesus' body was buried in great haste—so much so that it was not anointed in the customary way. The three named women, therefore, take the first available chance to complete the burial rituals.

But what they find at the tomb is astonishing. The huge stone closing it has been rolled away, and the place where the body had been laid is empty. They see an angel, who gives them a quite extraordinary message: Jesus 'has been raised'. The particular way the text phrases 'has been raised' (in the passive voice) implies that he has been raised by God. Moreover, he is 'going ahead' of them into Galilee, just as he had foretold on the night of his arrest (see page 86). This vision and message leave the women bewildered; they flee, and say nothing to anyone, 'because they were afraid.'

On this extraordinary note, the entire Gospel comes to an end. Why did the evangelist conclude his book in this surprising way? The most satisfactory answer seems to be that he deliberately chose to conclude his book in an open-ended way, leaving readers in suspense. What had happened (he seems to imply) is so mind-shattering that it cannot be expressed any further in words: you, the readers, will have to come to your own conclusions as to what this all means.

But we are not entirely taken by surprise by this ending. Jesus had clearly predicted that he would be handed over to the Gentiles and killed. And we have seen how all this did indeed come about. But the same prediction goes on, 'Three days later he will rise'. So we are hardly surprised to notice that the story on this page happens (on the ancient method of reckoning time) precisely three days after Jesus' death. Thus the earlier part of the Gospel has tried to prepare us for this bewildering ending.

The women, for their part, left the scene completely awestruck: were they witnessing the dawning of the New Age? Had the kingdom of God now actually come?

■ *a young man dressed in a white robe* This seems to be a typical way of describing the appearance of an angel.
■ *because they were afraid* The most ancient and reliable of the Greek manuscripts of the gospel text end at this point. Later manuscripts, however, add concluding paragraphs, though they differ amongst themselves greatly as to the wording.